Spiritual
Beef Broth
in a *Cup*

Spiritual
Beef Broth
in a Cup

90 Sustaining Devotions
for the Christian Under Pressure

Anna Noa Grace

Gentle Warrior
BOOKS

Published by Gentle Warrior Books

ISBN: 978-1-950685-45-5 (sc)

I dedicate this book to my children. I dedicate it to my friend Brent who has taught me so much. I dedicate it to my friend Minerva who encouraged me when I began to write it, and I dedicate it to Sharla who told me people want to read what I write.

Special thanks go to Chris Swanson for his inspiration, and to my best friend Rachel who was with me through it all. Thank you, Rachel!

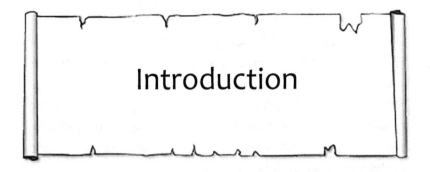

Introduction

I was conceived in depression, born in depression, nursed on depression and for the first 25 years of my life, lived depressed until God delivered me of it. I had moments of joy, but my default setting was depression. I have always had a knowing inside of me that there is something more. If life here is a pit and God is a good God, then that goodness tells me that what I have is not all that there is. The goodness tells me to reach out for it. The Creator of me is the Creator of it all and He IS good. He calls me into a purpose that brings goodness down . . . to me.

I need it.

He knows this.

John 1:14 ~ "The Word was made flesh, and dwelt among us . . ." Jesus is here, speaking still.

John 6:63 ~ "The words I speak unto you, they are spirit, and they are life." His word, spoken to us, becomes spirit—literally— and that spirit gives life.

Sometimes we find ourselves in a trial of our own doing. We know we've gone wrong. But sometimes we are just handed a raw deal—the trial of a lifetime!

The Bible has much to say about where God is in vicinity to the broken hearted. "The Lord is near to the brokenhearted and saves the crushed in spirit" (Psalm 34:18 ESV).

Dear one, if you feel crushed and in need of strength—whether you decide to believe God for the restoration of your relationships, or whether God leads you out of a destructive one—this devotional will walk you through the valley you have been driven into. The art pages are for your enjoyment. Feel free to color them, doodle on them, make notes, expand the pictures, paint, or do nothing at all. Each devotional stands on its own and can be studied in sequence or in any order.

Your purpose in this life is to be who He made YOU to be, not who a destructive one has told you to be. God has many things to teach us. Like beef broth, His word is rich with nutrients that will help you find your feet. Sometimes we use our feet to take a stand. Sometimes we use our feet to take a walk. But when life has knocked you to the ground, you first need to get on your feet.

I invite you to come on a journey with me. Let's spend some time with the Master Chef and see what He has in store for us.

Each devotional is designed to be the deep, rich nourishment you need to get through the hard trials in your life. Pull up a chair. Breathe in the aroma. God has been in the kitchen.

Anna Noa Grace

Go West

There once was a man, sitting alone on a small hill. There were bushes all around. Not tall trees, just shrubbery and bushes. There he sat all alone and sad. I'm going to take a walk, he thought. And he did. Presently he came to a cross. *The* cross. He had a full salvation experience. The joy and forgiveness he found were true and real.

Later, as he was letting his horse graze, he sat there pondering. How did I find this amazing cross? This cross that had the power to lift my burdens? This cross that gave me such hope? He thought back over that evening. He imagined the little knoll he had been sitting on. He saw again the setting sun and thought to himself, I know! I remember what I did! I walked toward that setting sun. I walked westward! That's it! The answer to all my life's problems came to me when I started to walk west!!

Suddenly, he felt inspired! He called his horse, saddled him, and began his tour of evangelism. "Go west!!" he shouted as he rode around the countryside. Whether someone was within hearing or not, he continued to ride and shout, "Go west!! The answer is to go west!! Are you burdened? Go west!! Are you lost? Go west!!"

A sad, young girl heard the Cryer and took his advice. She walked and walked and walked. She climbed over mountains, crossed streams and rivers, fought her way through jungles. She nearly died, several times, as she crossed the parched deserts. She was chased by a pack of wolves in the mountains. She was nearly drowned when she crossed the ocean. She desperately hung onto the hope that the Cryer was correct and that the cross would soon be seen. On and on she stumbled until she had circled the whole globe and was back again, to her own homeland. Finally about half a mile farther east of where she had been sitting when she had first heard the Cryer, she found the long-awaited cross. She fell in exhaustion at the foot of that cross. She cried and cried. The Lord met her there and finally, at last, she has her answer.

The gallant Cryer was still crying, "Go west!!! Keep going west!! There are still sinners that haven't found the cross."

The young girl heard the Cryer and was confused. *Go west?* she thought. *NO! I'm not going west!! I found my answer. I'm staying RIGHT HERE! The peace and rest I found in the cross is not to be taken away!* She wouldn't have it! She argued back to the Cryer, "You don't understand! I went through hell to get to where I am. Stop telling me to keep going west." But the Cryer, also sticking with his experience, insisted that the way to peace is west!

The point of this story is that sometimes people have an experience and they think others have to come to Jesus *the same direction* as they did. Whether it's a marriage in trouble, or a person stuck in a co-dependent situation, or a struggle with a person who has an opposite personality, as well as coming to Christ originally, people can exact an undue amount of "requirements" on others if they're not careful. This girl was already too far west! Going west, to her, meant nearly dying a hundred times and suffering unspeakable things. When really, what she needed to do was go a little east. Depending on where you are coming *from*, you may, or may not, need more or less of a thing.

Notes

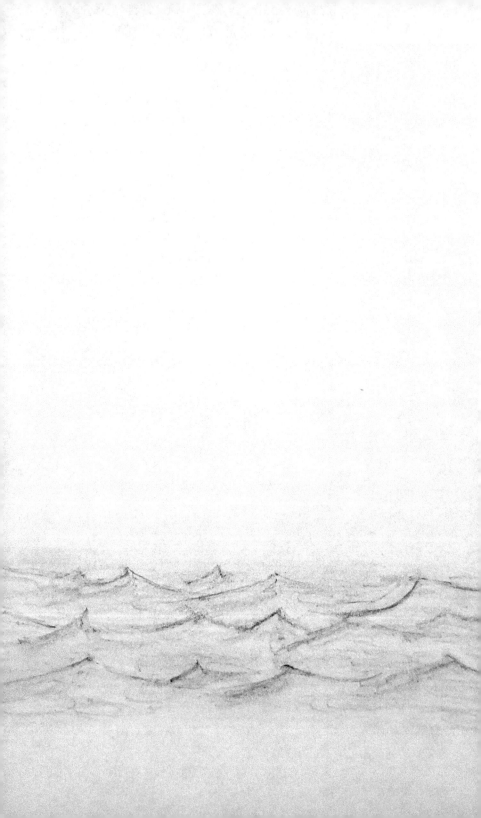

In the Beginning

One day as I was sitting in a church service, with my Bible open across my lap, I read "In the beginning, God . . ." in Genesis 1:1.

I was listening to my pastor preaching and my eyes rested on those words: "In the beginning, God..."

Still, paying more attention to what my pastor was saying than to what I was reading, my eyes scanned down the page, taking in the first words of each verse. Suddenly I could no longer hear my pastor. I was lost in the words of Genesis chapter one. Ponder with me.

"In the beginning, God . . ."

"And the earth was . . ."

"And God said . . ."

"And God saw . . ."

"And God called . . ."

"And God said . . ."

"And God made . . ."

"And God called . . ."

"And God said . . ."

"And God called . . ."

"And God said . . ."

And finally in verse 12—"And the earth brought . . ."

In the very beginning of Genesis—the first book of the Bible - He gives us a picture of how He deals with us. In the beginning— before there was anything, there was God. We're made of the dust of the earth, and when I was absentmindedly scanning the page, my eyes saw the word earth, but my mind saw us. We didn't "find God." *He* found *us! He* made *us!* This point alone is something that I need to remember from time to time when I'm tempted to "advise" God on how to run His universe.

So, in the beginning, God.

Then us.

In verses 3 to 11 I saw a picture of how He deals with us; gently.

"He said . . ."

When I was born, He said some things. I wonder what He said of me. It says, "He said."

Verse 4; "He saw . . . " We weren't lost in the crowd, or fallen through the cracks. He saw. He saw when I was two and left alone for hours. He saw when my family humiliated me. He saw when I got an A on my math test. When no one else saw, He saw.

"And God called..." When He called, He said some things. What did He say when He called you? I know some things He said to me. I told Him I couldn't. I told Him I was afraid.

"And God made..." Wow, did He ever! He made a way! He made some courage and gave it to me as a gift. He made me a better person when I could not do it myself. He made.

"And God called..."

"And God said..."

"And God called..."

"And God said..."

Each time He drew me closer to Him. It was hard to trust at first. I had no context to know trust like that. But, gently, per-sistently, He called me in and said things to me.

Verse 12; "And the earth brought..." What is it you need to

bring to God? As He called me closer and spoke with me, I began to see what I needed to bring. Hunger. Mostly I needed to bring my hunger. He gave me trust. And through this dance of calling, speaking, and coming close, we can finally bring it. First to Him. Then, together with Him, we bring it to the world around us. Our homes. Our families. Our communities and to the greater world.

I was no longer in the sanctuary of our little church. I had gone on a long journey. With God. He showed me many things as my eyes stared at the page open in my lap. He showed me that this is also how He deals with the ones I was praying for. I don't know how long it will take for each of them to dance this dance and finally come in. But, in the beginning, God.

God loved these people before I knew them. He calls, He speaks. He makes.

And the earth brings.

Prayer: Lord, I'm hungry. I bring to You my empty cup. Fill it with the deep, savory broth of Your rich Word. I will sip and be satisfied. Speak and I will listen. My heart is full of a lot of things. I will bring You one thing at a time and I will listen for You to speak. To call, to speak and to make.

Revelation 21:5 "And He that sat upon the throne said, Behold, I make all things new."

Access to Mercy

Hebrews 10:19-22 (KJV)
"Having therefore, brethren, boldness to enter into the holiest by the blood of Jesus, by a new and living way, which He hath consecrated for us, through the veil, that is to say, His flesh...let us draw near..."

I was reading this the other day and saw a thing I had never seen before. At the risk of boring you with the background story, let me just briefly explain a thing that began in the days of Moses.

The Tabernacle, the movable tent, was first set up in the wilderness and God gave minute, detailed instructions on the operations of the sacrifices performed there. This Tabernacle was later made into a permanent structure called the Temple. One of the many sacred details of the Tabernacle and Temple was a veil, a curtain, that was to separate the most holy room from the rest. Within this sacred room were articles God had instructed to be placed there, and it was to be the room into which God came to meet with the priest. There are already entire books written about this and for the mere sake of keeping it short, I will mention this one important part. Only a certain priest could do the work in this room, and if he didn't do his job properly in this sacred, curtained-off room, he would literally die in God's presence there. NO one else was EVER allowed to go in there, OR touch anything that belonged in there.

While I was reading Hebrews 10 that day, I saw an image of Jesus, standing in the Tabernacle, in the doorway of the holiest place. I saw His long flowing robe. I saw the priest going through the "veil" into the holiest place.

I knew the story well. On the day He was crucified, Jesus declared, "It is finished!" (John 19:30). And Matthew tells us, "Jesus cried out again with a loud voice, and gave up His spirit. Just then the Temple curtain was torn in two from top to bottom. The earth shook and the rocks were split apart" (Matt. 27:50-51 NET).

I saw that when Jesus was on the cross and the veil was *torn*, and He said, "It is finished," it was like He was set free of having to stand there PREVENTING and could now run out and GATHER!

The justice of God and the His heart of Mercy met and *exploded!* The veil was rent from top to bottom, the earth quaked, and rocks split open! (It was a big deal!) The explosion was the collision of justice and mercy.

Jesus was the veil. He still is. He still is the door. But the thing is, He is the DOOR—a door open! No longer does the Mercy of God have to be veiled and hidden...and prevented. The door swings open! Access to Mercy!

Prayer: Thank you Jesus for this access to mercy! Gather *me* today! I am Yours already, but gather me unto Yourself and talk to me. Tell me the things I need to know today. Fill me with Your merciful love.

Notes

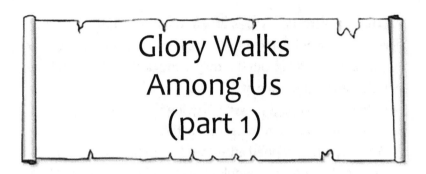

Glory Walks Among Us (part 1)

Luke 24:26 (KJV)
"Ought not Christ to have suffered these things, and to enter into His glory?"

The sun shone hot on the drooping shoulders of the two men as they walked the long stretch of road. The road was covered with pebbles and sand like all the other roads, but the two men hardly noticed. The bright sunshine seemed only to add insults to their sorrow. Why was the sun shining? Their world had just ended. They felt the sun had no right to be in the sky that had just fallen on them so miserably a few days ago.

The two talked as they walked, too numb for tears. How, really, would they go on living after losing the very Hope of Israel? They couldn't make sense of the story their friend Mary had told them either. Who in their whole region had the authority to move His body?! Their own double-dealing government must have pulled this con-job. Nothing was working out the way they had planned. Nothing.

Their conversation was as slow as their footsteps. Other travelers caught up with and passed them the whole trudging hour they had been walking, but this they didn't notice either, until one man slowed his pace to match theirs.

"Hey, what's up, guys? What's going on? You're deep in conversation and you seem so heavyhearted."

The two men stopped and stared a moment, not sure how to answer. Who on earth wouldn't already know what had happened? Was he mocking them like the sun in the sky seemed to be? The man with the question looked sincere. The two looked at each other. One of them voiced the questions, "Are you new here? Don't you know what happened?"

"What happened?"

It seemed they all three just had questions, so the two men filled in the parts they thought were most important. They had been introduced to a man named Jesus. A powerful man of God, in word and deed. But the top guys couldn't tolerate him, so they had him be put to a torturous death.

"We thought Jesus would never let this happen. We totally believed he was the Redeemer we had all been waiting for. What's more, the women told us this morning that the body is no longer in the tomb where we put it! It feels like our whole world has crashed down on us, and we have no idea what to do now."

The man called them foolish, but his eyes were full of compassion. He listened to their story, and then he spoke. He spoke for a long time. In fact, they had reached the next village before he was through. He explained a lot of things in the scriptures and showed them that the Redeemer had to suffer these things and enter into His glory.

When they reached the village, their new friend was going to walk on, but they were interested in hearing more. "Please stay here for the night. We can grab something to eat on the way to the motel. We would like to hear more of your interpretation of scripture."

The man agreed and when they were comfortably settled in the motel room, they unwrapped the sandwiches, eager to continue the conversation. The man held his sandwich and gave thanks to God before he took a bite.

The two men turned and stared at each other, wide-eyed and covered in goosebumps. They couldn't speak. Was this...? Is this...?

They both turned in unison to ask the man if he was Jesus, but he had literally disappeared, right in front of them!

"Dude! What just happened?!"

The whole idea of sleeping seemed irrelevant. Neither of them could remember later whether they ate their sandwiches or threw them in the trash. They could think of only one thing— to get back to Jerusalem to tell the disciples what they had just seen and heard.

Prayer: Walk with me today and teach me out of Your Word what I need to know today.

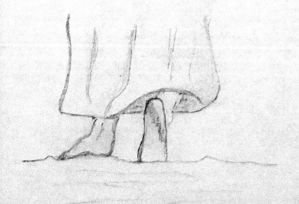

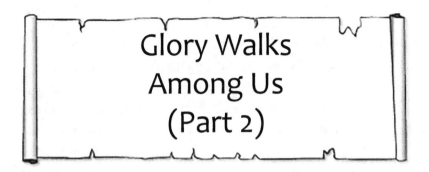

Glory Walks Among Us (Part 2)

Luke 24:26 (KJV)
"Ought not Christ to have suffered these things, and to enter into His glory?"

In an extended study on glory I came across two verses: John 2:11 and Luke 24:26. "This beginning of miracles (turning water to wine) did Jesus in Cana of Galilee and manifested forth His glory and His disciples believed on Him" (John 2:11 KJV). "Ought not Christ to have suffered these things, and to enter into His glory?" (Luke 24:26 KJV).

I'm told that the Western culture thinks in linear terms, so maybe it's natural that we read a verse like Luke 24:26 and see it as: Jesus suffered for 33 years, then, He went back to heaven, to glory. And we tend to think that we suffer on earth, then, later, we go to heaven, to glory.

While it's true that we later go to heaven, Jesus, our example, the One whom we are to imitate, and follow, "manifested forth His glory" *here*.

Toots, if we read Luke 24:26 as a sequential line of events, then glory is heaven. If we read it as simultaneous conditions, then we suffer *while also* manifesting His glory. John 16:33 promises that we will have pressure, oppression, afflictions, distress, and burdens. Can we *in the midst* of these things, turn our eyes to Jesus and search for ways *in the midst of* suffering to manifest forth His glory? Can we cease to "wait until the storm blows away" before we lift our heads? Can we lift our head to look for victory right in the middle of our painful experience? I believe we can, because we are warriors—gentle warriors, but we *are* warriors—and He came to make a way for us. Lift your head, Gentle Warrior. You were made for this.

We are His glorious inheritance (Eph. 1:18) *while we are still here.* Christ is seated "far above all . . . not only in this world (hence, *in this world*) but also in that which is to come" (Eph. 1:21 KJV). "God raised us up with Christ and seated us with Him in the heavenly realms in Christ Jesus" (Eph. 2:6 NIV).

The best revenge on suffering is to walk the length of it, slaying dragons the whole way through it.

Prayer: Lift up my head, Lord. When I am too weak to lift it myself or too overwhelmed to see the good in the future, lift my head.

Oh Lord, how many are my foes! Many are rising against me; many are saying of my soul, "There is no salvation for him in God." But You, O Lord, are a shield about me, my glory, and the lifter of my head. Psalm 3:1-3 (ESV)

Notes

Make It
Personal

Psalm 119:105 (KJV)
"Thy Word is a lamp unto my feet, and a light unto my path."

"If Your law had not been *my* delight, then *I* would have perished in my affliction" (Ps. 119:92 NASB emphasis added)

"Thou, through Thy commandments, has made *me* wiser that mine enemies: for they are ever with *me*." (Ps. 119:98 KJV emphasis added)

"Thy Word is a lamp unto *my* feet, and a light unto *my* path." (Ps. 119:105 KJV emphasis added)

"The wicked have set their traps for *me* along Your path, but *I* will not turn from Your commandments." (Ps119:110 NLT emphasis added)

Make it personal.

The wicked have laid traps since the beginning, even in the Garden of Eden! In all the generations since the first one, we have had to be vigilant and aware. *And* not surprised when we suffer afflictions. If our concept of a good life is a life of no obstructions, no accidents, no perils, then I'm sorry, but we will be endlessly disappointed because in this life that's just not the case!

My focus needs to be to consume the Word and train my spirit to hear His voice *so that* when I encounter the ambush of the enemy, God's light illuminates *my* path. Be assured. There will be enemies! There will be traps. The way to beat the enemy at his game is to actively immerse myself in the Word of God, seek His face, and hear His voice. Need light? Read, read, read. His Word IS the light. Don't be caught in the dark. Make it personal.

If you run with a group that reads and applies the light, you might have enough light to walk by, but the Word says, "Thy Word is a lamp unto *my* feet, and a light unto *my* path." Notice what it does *not* say. It doesn't say Thy Word is a lamp unto my father's path, and therefore I will walk on his path. It doesn't say Thy Word is a lamp unto my friend's path; therefore I will walk on my friend's path. We can't walk someone else's path and live vicariously through others' lives (See Matthew 25). Make it personal.

Do you know your path? Do you know what the Lord has called you to walk out? Be not afraid. His light will light the way. His Word will not lead you astray. If I reach a section of my life's path that is extremely dangerous and treacherous, I can learn a lot from my friend's example as she walks her path, but I have to make it personal and live the life that God has given to *me*.

Prayer: Sustain me according to Your Word, that I may live, and do not let me be ashamed of my hope (Psalm 119:116).

Notes

Have You
Not Heard?

Isaiah 40:28 (KJV)
"Hast thou not known? Hast thou not heard? The everlasting God, the Lord, the Creator of the ends of the earth, faintest not, neither is weary."

I've experienced the incredible heaviness that comes with the lie that God doesn't care or know about the condition of my life. In verse 27 of this chapter, Jacob is complaining. He said that his way is hidden from the Lord and that God has disregarded his cause. This is as heavy as gloom.

"He sits enthroned above the circle of the earth" (Isaiah 40:22 NIV). Sometimes He seems that far away! That aloof to what is going on in my world.

But have you not heard? No. Sometimes I have not heard. The part of me that feels like God Himself has turned a deaf ear to me, has not heard. When real life crises seem to blot out everything we thought was true, and we feel like God has abandoned us, our souls are starved. Faint. We need nourishment. That's when, my dear friend, we go on a hunt. The enemy has robbed that cupboard bare and we need to go in search of sustenance.

What is God's opinion of people mistreating each other? "The Lord looked and was displeased that there was no justice. He saw that there was no one, He was appalled that there was no one to intervene" (Isaiah 59:15b–16a NIV). *That's* what God thinks!

Truth is the greatest antidote to a lie. This sounds elementary, but when our hearts are buried under a full load of depression, we need the authentic, foundational Word of God to tunnel its way through to us. The lie says that God neither sees nor cares about what I'm going through, but God's Word says otherwise.

"Do you not know? Have you not heard? The Lord is the everlasting God, the Creator of the ends of the earth. He will not grow tired or weary, and His understanding no one can fathom. He gives strength to the weary, and increases the power of the weak. Even youths grow tired and weary, and young men stumble and fall; but those who hope in the Lord will renew their strength. They will soar on wings like eagles; they will run and not grow weary, they will walk and not be faint" (Isaiah 40:28–31 NIV).

God does see. We might be tired, but He is not! It's easy to believe the lie that God doesn't understand what we go through, but the truth is that WE don't understand, and to transfer our own inability to understand onto God is a bit like putting ourselves in His shoes. That's too much for us. We cannot be our own god. The Word says that HE will give strength to the weary.

The Redeemer will come. That's a promise. Today, if you feel forgotten, let me recommend that you get out a large bowl. The Word says "those who hope in the Lord." To hope is to bring your large bowl before the Lord. Fight the lie. Bring the hope—the expectancy to receive—and He will very certainly pour into your bowl. The broth—the words—that He pours will truly renew your strength.

Prayer: Oh Lord God, the self-existent, eternal Holy One, You alone are God. Today I will believe. I am small and my understanding is limited, but You are able to do far exceeding above what I can imagine with my mind. Forgive my doubt and fill my bowl today with the riches of your glory. Strengthen my soul through Your Spirit, and give me the faith to be rooted in Your love. (*paraphrased prayer from Ephesians 3:14–21*)

Notes

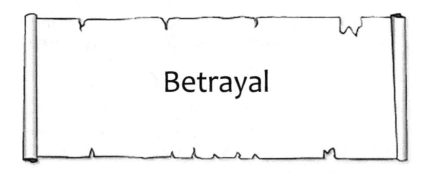

Betrayal

Proverbs 20:5 (ESV)
"The purpose in a man's heart is like deep water, but a man of understanding will draw it out."

True confessions of a wounded warrior: The words that Jesus loves me and has a plan for my life were hard to believe. How could He love and want me? No one else did. If He loved me, it would be out of pity because I thought it would have, after all, been better that I had not been born.

There were many times in my young life that I wished I was never born. In fact, the words, "it would have been better if I'd never been born" were a constant mantra in my head. When at various times in my adolescence, someone would try to "talk me out of" a depression, I felt like they were lying to me. Looking back, I see now that they *didn't* know what they were saying to me. At least they didn't know how to help me. Not really. I needed a deeper truth because the mantra kept playing in my head.

No worries. Jesus has since redeemed me, but this is the reality I come from. Redemption. Thank God for redemption!

Listen to Matthew 26:24— "Woe to the man by whom the Son of Man is betrayed! It would have been better for that man if he had not been born" (ESV). There was a man of whom it truly could be said that it would have been better if he had not been born. Betrayal is that vicious.

When *we* hear the message that it would have been better if we had not been born, where is it coming *from*? What did Judas do? He linked with Satan to *betray* Jesus! What is Satan's *motive* in coming to us with the message that it would have been better if we were never born?

Betrayal.

Our agreement with Satan is betrayal to our Redeemer. Any time we agree with a lie, it locks us into the pain and the consequences of it (the lie). In my ignorance and the circumstances I was born into, I didn't know any other truth and believed the words in my head. My agreement with them reaped the *feelings* of betrayal—that the whole universe had robbed *me!* Robbed me of life and meaning. Hence the *purpose* of the words were to *produce* betrayal.

My journey out of that abyss needed a truth that could set me free. I needed more than words. I needed to repent of making an agreement with Satan before I could be free of the consequences. Thank GOD that He came for me! Thank God that there IS redemption and freedom. But mere words are not always enough. Sometimes knowledge of the truth and a breaking of agreement is necessary—then comes the freedom. And in freedom comes purpose. And our purpose is achieved in life. This life. On the North side of the grass!

Little wonder that our enemy first wants us to agree that we should not have been born. It kicks open the door for him to come in and defeat our Purpose. What a premeditating shark!

The words were true for Judas but were not meant for me! I was tuning in to the wrong network! We are given choices. The cross gave us choices. We now choose whether to betray Jesus or choose to break our allegiance to the Betrayer and live out our eternal Purpose.

Do you identify with this message of betrayal and redemption? For today's prayer, I encourage you to scan through your own life. The Lord can reveal to you what still holds you captive. He is The Redeemer and I trust that He will lead you on.

Notes

Commander

Joshua 5:13 (NIV)
"Now when Joshua was near Jericho, he looked up and saw a man standing in front of him with a drawn sword in his hand. Joshua went up to him and asked, 'Are you for us or for our enemies?'"

In the early years of development, a child's perception is programmed without the child being aware of the program. It has been my experience that when we have been mistreated, abused, and otherwise trained that people are malicious, we react in one of two ways—or a little of both: one being an unyielding mistrust of everyone, and the other being an excessive confidence in our own judgment, both of which are enormous obstacles in our path to freedom.

Joshua, well on his way to freedom, encountered a man with a message for him. He had a typical response of immediately bristling—the fight or flight reflex. I mean, to Joshua's credit, the man in his path did have a sword. Drawn. But as is often the case with the wounded race, he instinctively bristled, ready to fight. Most of our inclinations to do so are honestly earned. We have legitimate reasons for hostility, or mistrust, or an inability to trust anyone but ourselves. This reaction presents scads of difficulty in human relationships and in our one most important relationship—ours with our Lord.

We might have had to rely on our own grit so long, it feels like the safest option. People might have tormented us to so many years that to trust seems to be a trap. The Promised Land can represent many things. If I were to begin to name them all, I would unwittingly leave out important ones. In the case of The Promised Land representing our freedom from bondage and our entry into our position as overcomer and receiver of promised victory, there is something we must establish before we fight the very One who came to set us free. (And fight off the messengers He sends to lead us into victory.)

When Joshua asked the man if he was for Israel or for their enemies, the man replied, "Neither. I am the Commander of the army of the Lord. I am not here for you or against you. I'm here as Captain." See, when we've lived a long time protecting ourselves, we can see others as threats. We automatically assess everyone as "on our side" or "against us." That's a stressful way to live! It puts a lot of strain on our relationships. Eventually it pushes everyone away.

At some point before we enter a Promised Land of kingdom authority and victorious living, we have to (Josh. 5:14) fall face-down to the ground in reverence and ask the Captain, the Lord, what message He has for His servant. In other words, surrender. In the Kingdom we don't gain authority by pushing and shoving our way to the top. We gain authority as we surrender to His authority.

"Are you for us or for our enemies?"

"Neither. But as commander of the army of the Lord I have now come." (Josh. 5:13-14 NIV)

In the very applicable imagery of Israel crossing the expanse from Egypt (sin and bondage) to the Promised Land (salvation and freedom from bondage) Joshua was already well on his way. It's not about us being "bad" or "good" or even "better than I used to be." It's about noticing when it's time to surrender to God. When He blocks your way with a raised sword, it's a good time to adjust your self-dependence and consider that maybe you don't call the shots. He does. Obey. Follow Him.

Prayer: Lord, what message do You have for Your servant today?

Notes

First, the Relationship

Hebrews 3:7-8 (NIV)
"So as the Holy Spirit says, 'Today if you hear His voice, do not harden your hearts as you did in the rebellion, during the time of testing in the desert.'"

For some people Fall is a favorite time of year. I personally prefer Springtime when things are bursting open with new life and bright colors. But it was one day in September that He spoke to me about hardness of heart. In the Northern hemisphere, September is the time when things are beginning to shut down, close, harden, and go to sleep. The visual was right in front of me.

The story in Hebrews, from where today's verse comes, is a story about the people of God in the desert. For forty years they saw what He did. Yet, they tested God until He became angry. Verses 10 and 11: "I was angry with that generation, and I said, 'Their hearts are always going astray and they have not known My ways.' So I declared an oath in my anger, 'They shall never enter my rest!'"

I noticed a few things. One, it's possible to (verse 9) see for forty years what God does and still not know His ways. And two, hardening your heart is a sin.

Why do we harden our hearts at times?

The Hickory, Oak, and Walnut trees around our house form a very hard shell around their seeds—to protect the seeds during the long winter months. Could I suggest to you that we are attempting our own form of self-protection when we harden our hearts.

I noticed that God considers a hardened heart a rebellious heart. A heart that hasn't known His ways.

He wants to be known.

To know and be known; one of our deepest core needs.

The angry oath of God was, "They shall never enter my rest!" To know Him is to find rest. We find rest when we know His ways. Our hearts desperately need this relationship. In the peace of His rest—knowing Him and being known by Him—we have nothing to prove. Living our lives like we had nothing to prove is not like the death and dying scenes I saw outside my window. The leaves on my trees were turning crispy, giving up, and falling to the ground.

Our human nature might be inclined to believe that to lay down our need to prove our point is equal to giving up and falling into decay on the ground. But not so.

We can't manufacture peace. First, the relationship. The knowing and being known. Then the rest. And only from that place of rest comes the surrender into His ways. And in His ways we know who we are and we have no need to harden our heart in a human attempt to self-preserve. Manufactured peace ends up in decay on the ground. But being secure in God we are snuggly wrapped up in His peace, ready for new growth.

Prayer: Show me one thing, Lord, that I can change today to adjust my attitude to put relationship first. Show me a place where I have been shutting my own heart down. I want to know You and be known. I want to step into more rest and I want to feel peace regardless of today's storm.

Notes

Child of the Free Woman

Galatians 4:31 (NIV)
"Therefore brothers and sisters, we are not children of the slave woman, but of the free woman."

One year we lived in makeshift living quarters in a large garage. It was in this less agreeable living arrangement that I came across a revelation of Galatians 4. In verse 24 it says, "These things are being taken figuratively: The women represent two covenants."

Maybe it was my primitive living arrangement. Maybe it was the other rotten situation in my life at the time. Whatever the cause, this day, with my two parakeet birds keeping watch of my study, I read chapter 4 and my eyes opened to a whole new way of seeing things. The two women in this passage were, of course, Hagar and Sarah, and much could be written about those two. The writer of Galatians says they represent two covenants. He also says one is of the flesh and the other is of the promise. One is "born of slavery" and one is "born of divine Promise."

I saw a thought process. One thought process leads to slavery, enslavement. One thought process leads to freedom, empowerment. I may not have gotten much done that morning as far as house work goes! I was engrossed in my study of this concept! I was captivated.

In the same way as a single cell is a tiny replica of the whole, so is the story of these two women a replica of a whole concept. In the two sides of an argument in our own head, one leads to bondage or death and one leads to freedom and life. The choice is presented to us every day. Am I going to think like a defeated, enslaved victim or am I going to think like an empowered, conquering child of the divine Promise?

Am I going to look on the dark side? Am I going to believe? Am I going to doubt? Did God give me a promise of divine order? Am I going to let doubts and sorrow enslave my mind and take me back into the bondage I was released from? Or am I going to live in faith that He will see me through?

"Now you, brothers and sisters, like Isaac, are children of promise. At that time the son born according to the flesh persecuted the son born by the power of the Spirit. It is the same now" (Galatians 4:28-29 NIV).

Is it ever! Always. All day long! The struggle is real.

"What does the Scripture say? 'Get rid of the slave woman and her son, for the slave woman's son will never share in the inheritance with the free woman's son!'" (verse 30)

For me, that day, in my archaic living quarters, I saw this "slave woman and her son" as the rotten thoughts and all the thoughts birthed out of my original rotten thought! Get rid of them! Throw them OUT! Those enslaved ways of thinking won't ever have a share in the promised end that God has spoken to me and thinking rotten thoughts is not going to get me to the end I desire.

I stood up and declared to the whole garage and to my parakeet birds that were listening from their cage, "We are NOT children of the slave woman, but of the FREE woman!!"

The parakeets didn't seem to care, but they did stop their chatter for a moment to listen.

Sweetums, listen to me. We have got to grab hold of this concept if we are going to win at this! The thoughts we think determine the destination. Don't think for a moment there isn't a real war going on for the control of your mind! If your mind is a cupboard where you store things to think about, it would be wise to do inventory and throw out the ingredients that will keep you enslaved.

Prayer: Jesus, You gave Yourself to redeem me from this present evil. Take my hand and lead me to freedom. Lead me to life. Wash my mind. Make me clean. Make me new. Feed me the truth. Strengthen my mind to win against these sons-of-slaves thoughts that persecute me! I want You, Jesus. I want to be free; I want truth.

Notes

Of Dust
and Word

1 Corinthians 6:17 (KJV)
"But he that is joined unto the Lord is one spirit."

Today I'd like to take you on a little walk through the pages of Scripture. A bit of a treasure hunt. Grab your Bible and come with me. The first stop will be Genesis 2:7.

"And the Lord God formed man of the dust of the ground and breathed into his nostrils the breath of life." (KJV)

We know the scenery well. The Lord God made Adam. Adam and Eve chose to eat the fuzzy kiwi. God put them out of the garden. On our walk through the story we'll stop and read Genesis 3:19. "[In consequence to Adam's sin, God said] In the sweat of thy face shalt thou eat bread, till thou return unto the ground; for out of it wast thou taken, for dust thou art and unto dust shalt thou return." (KJV)

The Lord God made us from dust and to dust we shall return. Ok, got it. Moving on to the book of John we find that "In the beginning was the Word, and the Word was with God, and the Word was God. In Him was life, and the life was the light of men. And the Word was made flesh and dwelt among us..." (John 1:1,4, and 14 KJV)

What was Jesus made of? Jesus came from the Word. Salvation came through Jesus. The Body of Christ was made by the Word of God. The part of us that is born again is not made of dust, but of the Word of God.

We are born of the Word! The very Light and Life of Jesus is in us. The Word has the power to create things that are not. (Hebrews 11:3)

Pause. Sit down beside the deep, deep well of who and what the Word is. We will face opposition in this world! That's a given! The part of us that is made of the Word is also made creative and powerful in that when we face the opposition, we don't bring our own power. We bring The Word. "He that is joined unto the Lord is one spirit." We are not on our own. We are joined with Him and born of Him. The Word was with God in the beginning. The creative, powerful Word of God now dwells within us. If you're going through or facing a hard time, I invite you to draw from this deep, deep well. Find what the Word says about the thing you're going through. Think it, speak it, declare it, pray it, live it. Do not let the enemy rob you of the rich wealth of the deep, deep Word of God. It is eternal and will not be made void. Ever. (Isaiah 55:11)

Prayer: I bow my knees unto You, Father, and ask that You grant me, according to the riches in glory, to be strengthened with might by Your Spirit in my inner person. In faith I ask that Christ may dwell in my heart and that I may be rooted and grounded in love. I ask to be able to comprehend how wide, how long, how deep and how high the love of God is in Christ—the love that passes beyond knowledge. I ask to be filled with all the fullness of God, Who is able to do exceedingly and abundantly more than all that I can ask or think, according to the power that is at work in me. Unto You, be the glory throughout all the ages, Amen. (Ephesians 3:14-21)

Notes

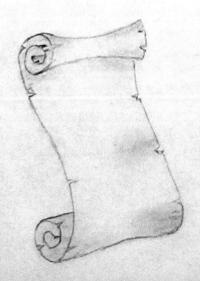

Give Ear

2 Chronicles 34:26-27 (BBE)

". . . to the king of Judah . . . This is what the Lord, the God of Israel, has said: Because you have given ear to my words, and your heart was soft, and you made yourself low before God on hearing His words about this place and its people, and with weeping and signs of grief have made yourself low before Me, I have given ear to you, says the Lord."

This place. Its people. We all get to "that place" full of "those people" from time to time. Sometimes "those people" are the ones we work with at our job. Sometimes they live in our home. Wherever "that place" is for you today, it is very likely that "its people" need God.

In Josiah's case, the people had "moved God to wrath by all the works of their hands." (verse 25) There is a reason we are moved to wrath when people work against us and against everything true and noble. God has those feelings, too. Earlier in the story in 2 Chronicles 34, King Josiah had given the command to clean up the damage that was done to the House of God. During the clean-up project the priest found The Book of the Law and some of it was read to the king. These are the words that moved the king to weeping and grief.

Someone once said that you can't receive from God with your heart clenched. Symbolically, we can't receive anything with our fists clenched shut.

We naturally feel anger when our space is violated. We're made in the image of God. God has emotion. We have emotion. To shut off emotion is not the answer. In the example of King Josiah, we can pour out to God those emotions. I've found in my life I can listen better once I've poured out the moldy stew that has been collecting bacteria for days.

Dear one, don't condemn yourself for having toxic emotions. Pour them all out before the Lord. You will then be able to give your ear to the words the Lord has to say. It's hard to humble our heart when it's pumped big and full of gaseous fumes. Pouring out the bad will make space for humbling.

Josiah's heart was soft and he gave his ear to God's words and God gave ear to Josiah's prayers.

Prayer: Today let the steam vent out until you can connect with a peace, a humbleness, before God. Listen for God's word about this place and its people. Pray from the soft place. God will hear you.

[James 1:19-25 is a great complement to today's message if you have time to explore and pray through it.]

Notes

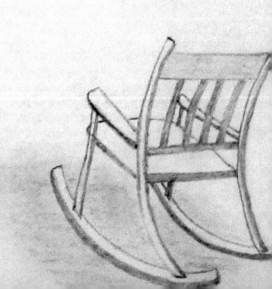

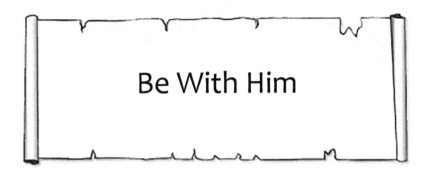

Be With Him

Mark 3:14 (KJV)
"And He ordained twelve, that they should be with Him and that He might send them forth to preach."

This fascinates me. We're called. We're chosen. We try. We fail. We wonder.

God, I thought you said...

But what *did* He say? He ordained the twelve that they should *be* with Him. What a gift! To hang out with Jesus. The sending, the preaching, the doing, the working comes. But it comes a-f-t-e-r the being.

How does it feel to you to have Jesus ask you just to be with Him?

Maybe you're both talking. Maybe you're both relaxed and quiet. Maybe He takes you somewhere and shows you something. Maybe He gives you a special gift. Whatever it is, it's time well spent.

Spending time in the peaceful Presence of Jesus is the first part of our calling.

In today's prayer time, I will not lead you. Let your imagination lead you. Feel the express joy of the Lord's invitation to simply *be* with Him.

Notes

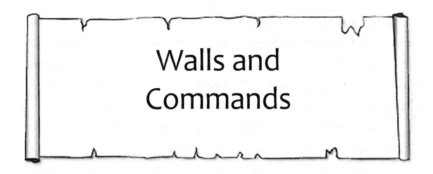

Walls and Commands

Joshua 5:14 (KJV)

"...And Joshua fell on his face on the earth, and did worship, and said unto him, 'What saith my lord unto his servant?'"

We all have our Jerichos, our Goliaths, our Rivers of Jordan, and we often find ourselves in the middle of a test we haven't studied for. Trials of our faith are called trials for a reason. If they were pieces of cake, they wouldn't be called trials. If we knew the answers, the trials wouldn't be as hard to navigate.

Recently as I was reading Joshua 5, I noticed verse 14. I might have noticed it because I saw myself in his shoes. They had just crossed the Jordan—a miracle of mammoth proportion—only to meet *another* insurmountable odd.

The Lord had already told Joshua not to fear, this land was going to belong to Israel. Joshua had the big picture, he just didn't know how exactly to proceed. Have you found yourself here? Perhaps you're in this place today. You have a big word from God, a big assignment. You *want* to obey and take the assignment on, but gosh, the enemy is right there, in your face!

Maybe you, like myself many times, find yourself in a bitter trial and you DON'T know what the assignment is. You're just in a trial and have no definitive word from God about it. I distinctly remember the season of time when the Lord began to train me to stop making demands. Like Joshua, I learned to sit before the Lord and ask, "What saith my Lord unto His servant?"

Compared to all of time, our life span is a puff of steam. A very important puff, but just a puff. I don't know it all. I know some things, but I am in no position whatsoever to be "telling" God what to do or how to lead me.

If we are to win our battle at all, we have to get humble before God and hush our mouth of all things except the words, "What do you want me to do?" Don't get me wrong. There is a time for battle. There is a time for everything (Ecclesiastes 3). But first—humility and silence before Almighty God. Sometimes the atmosphere is so cluttered we need to fast as well as seek.

If you're in a place like this, I encourage you, as long as it takes—get on your face and ask Him what he wants you to do. There have been times in my life when He spoke immediately. There have been times when I sought His face for thirty days before I heard His voice. Gentle Warrior, as long as it takes, we must clear the clutter in the air and the clutter in our hearts and get His commands.

Does it make sense to walk around a walled city for seven days in order to take the city? Some of the things the Lord will tell you to do will not make much sense. But if He says do it, do it.

Ezekiel 36:23 (NLT) "I will show how holy My great name is—the name you dishonored among the nations. And when I reveal My holiness through you before their very eyes, says the Sovereign Lord, then the nations will know that I am the Lord."

We are in our battles to win them—not for our own great name, but for His.

Prayer: Let today's prayer come from your own heart, from your unique situation, between you and God. Semper fi. You will win.

Notes

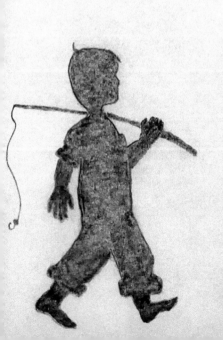

Displeased
or Healed

Zechariah 1:2 (KJV)
"The Lord hath been sore displeased with your fathers."

The Hebrew people have an interesting and colorful history of devotion and rebellion. People are people. The story of humanity is that we don't all get it right. I have learned so much about human relationships throughout the Old Testament.

Let me light a section of the path that led me to personal freedom by drawing our attention to the verse today. "The Lord hath been sore displeased with your fathers." Dear one, if your parents or caretakers were harmful humans, it's not your fault. They may have programmed you to absorb shame that isn't yours to carry. But you're no longer a child and as the adult that you are, you have permission to look at things the way they really were. God Himself is "sore displeased" with some people's behavior.

Sometimes life is hard because people around us are difficult. Sometimes life is hard because we're trying to do life without the proper tools. Throughout the Old Testament I find passages like this one in Zechariah that explain the emotions of God. I found freedom in understanding that emotions are part of how we are made in His image. A lifetime of suppressed emotion puts us in a great disadvantage.

I know for myself there was much misplaced guilt involved in looking truthfully at the events in my childhood. As children we're wired to look up to the adults in our lives. They, and our world with them, are all we know. As children we need the adults to be right. We need this so much that our small brains actually rewrite the events of our lives and we absorb the shame in order to let our parent be the good guy—and thus begins a life of dysfunction.

When we're wired to make the other person be right and ourselves wrong, it also "feels" wrong to correct this. But truly—if God is sore displeased, we can also be displeased. We don't have to continue on in the crippling bondage that keeps us afraid to feel what we feel.

These false shames are like parasites in the bowels. Even when we do take in the good, nourishing broth of the Word, if the "parasites" are in there, they say, "No, me first!" If we're unaware of the parasitic beliefs and programming, we will end up obeying them before we obey the Word. This also is sore displeasing to God.

Do you need freedom from this? There IS freedom from the POW camp of neglect and abuse! When you were a child, not every adult around you was wise. Follow the warrior Jesus and He will lead you through the maze of traps and pitfalls to your escape. He will show you what is garbage and what is truth. Your "fathers" may or may not all have listened to Him, but you can.

Each of our stories is complicated and completely unique, individually. Each of us navigate our own journey toward health and wholeness. Today's thought is designed simply to shed light on one small section of the journey. If our caretakers damaged our soul, we have permission to heal. We don't have to stay broken for fear of seeking and speaking the truth. Be assured that He is sore displeased that we were ever damaged in the first place.

"And the people...followed Him: and He received them, and spake unto them of the kingdom of God, and healed them that had need of healing." (Luke 9:11 KJV)

Prayer: Speak to me, Heavenly Father of your Kingdom. My programming is faulty and I need to understand how You do life in the Kingdom. Show me the false beliefs I still need to be freed of. Heal me of the damage they have done and teach me to walk in freedom. Give me the courage to face the truth and throw out the false guilt. Teach me which is which. I can't understand this on my own, but You will lead me out.

Notes

_____

_____

_____

_____

_____

_____

_____

_____

_____

The Level Place

Luke 6:17 (NIV)
"He went down with them and stood on a level place..."

The context is that He had just been to the mountain to pray. He prayed all night, and in the morning He called His disciples to Himself and He chose His twelve. He called them apostles—He assigned their life's calling to them. Then verse 17.

Today as I read these words, I'm inspired to notice that He went down, with them, and stood on a level place.

People who live with trauma, are in trauma, or have been in past trauma, know that nothing is level! In trauma the whole base we stand on is tilting and shaking like a trick stage. Everything appears to be mocking us, waiting for us to slide off and fall, fall, fall down, down to who knows what kind of mental insanity. We have things to say, we can't say them and won't be heard when we speak from this unstable place.

Jesus, the King of the Kingdom, the Healer of pain, stands with us. He's mindful of us. He stands with us until we know that we are known. Until we feel felt. He, the empathic Listener, holds space with us. Meets us where we are, speaks the Word that heals our wound. He *takes a stand* with us until finally, at long last, the place we stand holds still. He stands with us in a level place. For me this happened through people who ministered to me this way, with Him. He revealed many things to me on my own, but He also led me to people who knew how to help me. People who knew how to stand with me until the place we stood on held still.

Luke 6:17: "He went down with them and stood on a level place. A large crowd of His disciples was there and a great number of people from all over Judea, from Jerusalem, and from the coast of Tyre and Sidon." (NIV) In other words, He came down from the mountain to speak to the crowd. We have things to say. This leveling, the healing, the standing, the standing *up*, taking the role God gives, this is the place on which to speak from. The place itself speaks. The testimony of where He brought us from. The testimony of our healing. Our restoration. This place—this testimony—speaks volumes. From this place we can address the nations. (Isaiah 60:1-3)

Prayer: Thank you God that You don't leave us helpless. Lead me to the level place. I'm asking for all the steps involved between where I am now to where the level place is. Short or long, I want to be in that stable place with You. And I want to walk in the calling You have called me to.

Notes

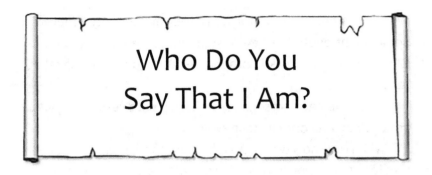

Who Do You Say That I Am?

Matthew 16:13–20 (NLT)

"Jesus asked 'Who do people say that I AM?'

'Well,' they replied, 'some say John the Baptist, some say Elijah, and others say Jeremiah or one of the prophets.'

Then He asked, **'Who do you say that I am?'**

Simon Peter answered, 'You are the Messiah, The Son of the **living God!'**

Jesus replied, 'You are **blessed**, Simon, son of John, because my **Father** in heaven has **revealed this to you!** You did not learn this **from any human being!** Now I say to you that you are Peter and upon this rock I will build my church, and **all the powers of hell will not conquer it.** And I will give you the keys of the Kingdom of Heaven. Whatever you forbid (bind) on earth will be forbidden in heaven and whatever you open on earth will be opened in heaven.

Then He sternly warned them not to tell anyone that He was the Messiah."

Acts 1:8 "But you will receive power when the Holy Spirit comes on you, and you will be my witnesses . . . to the ends of the earth."

✍

When you ask people who Jesus is, they might quote scripture. Some might quote the New Testament, some might quote the Old. Some might speak in prophesies. But who do you say that Jesus IS?

When we have personal experiences with Jesus we gain a strength that no one can take away.

When you know who Jesus is because the Father has revealed Him to you then you have a living knowledge of Him and it won't be that you've learned it from any human, and no devil in hell can take it from you.

The revelations that come when you seek Him and His word are yours.

You have the keys and will lock and unlock upon the earth what is in heaven.

Sometimes we're tempted to "share" these words with others. But Jesus cautioned Peter sternly, "Don't tell anyone."

What did He say? Depending on which translation we read, we get a slightly different spin on this verse. Here is what the Literal Translation says, "And I will give to you the keys of the kingdom of Heaven. And whatever you bind on earth shall occur, having been bound in Heaven. And whatever you may loose on the earth shall be, having been loosed in Heaven."

When the Lord Himself shows us what He has in the storeroom—in heaven—our first assignment is to bring it to earth. Prayer. As a married woman, instead of being a nagging, "sharing" wife, we first go to prayer. The battle is won in the Spirit first. Later we can watch our treasure walk on the earth. There are times when I have been able to speak God's word to my husband, but only after the Lord and I spent time planting and tending the seed.

If you're a man, as Peter was, remember the Lord told him He would build His church on the rock. The rock is to stand on, not throw. Establish a confident, dependable foundation and build people up.

"And when the Holy Spirit has come upon you, you will receive power and will be able to tell people..." (Acts 1 :8 paraphrased) When the time is right, you will feel the Holy Spirit upon you. When He says speak and we speak, the words are His words and not our own.

Prayer: Lord, I take a moment to agree with the Word. I need the strength of these personal revelations with You. Feed me and I will be strong. Show me and I will see. Walk with me and I will not faint.

Notes

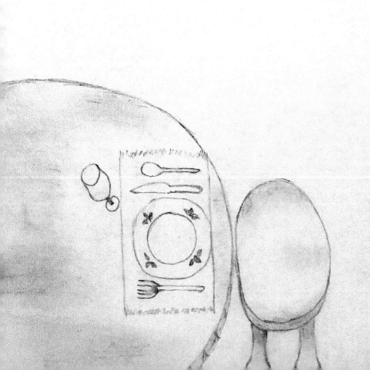

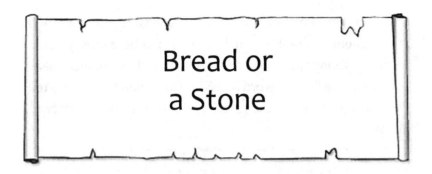

Bread or
a Stone

Matthew 7:9 (NIV)
"Which of you, if his son asks for bread, will give him a stone?"

A funny thing about deception is that if you were honestly deceived, you wouldn't know it. If you knew it and still believed the lie, we would have another word for it: Nonsense. When I was a young girl I pondered on this sneaky nature of deception.

If we were to picture a relationship looking like a tall building, we would see each layer of brick and steel being the days, months, and years of the relationship. At the end of a lifetime of friendship, we'd have a beautiful architectural structure, unique and stately, standing tall and solid with a personal touch of artistic display representing the many beautiful qualities of the friendship. Lies and deception in our metaphoric building project would be cardboard bricks. Foam pillars. Mashed potato mortar. What can be built on top of a layer of that?! Everything crumbles. Lies are not innocent. They're extremely destructive. To yourself. To your partner. To the "buildings" close by.

Matthew 7:7 (NIV) says, "Ask and it will be given to you; seek and you will find..." Young as I was, I took this promise. I made a covenant with the Lord that from His everlasting goodness and commitment to me, He would never let me be deceived. Ever. From this foundation, the Lord has built and established many truths into my life. His word is solid. Often when I have revisited this passage in my life the Lord has shown me another layer to discover.

One morning I sat staring at these words: "Which of you, if his son asks for bread, will give him a stone?" I thought, "That's me! I'm Your daughter! I asked for a covenant of truth between us!"

He took me back to the words, "asks for bread…"

"Yes, Lord. I know. Bread. Stone. You won't deceive us."

"No, you're not getting it."

"Getting what?"

"Read it again."

"…if his son asks for bread…"

Suddenly a flood of sights washed through my mind. The metaphor of bread runs back as far as Genesis! I read it again. "Which of you, if your son asks for bread, will give him a stone?"

"For the bread of God is He who comes down from heaven, and gives life to the world." (John 6:33 NIV) It would take a whole book to write about all the scenes running through my mind as I sat and pondered. One of the scenes I saw was Moses, stone tablets in hand, coming down from the mountain. I understood the exchange of covenants. The stone tablets looked to me like the unyielding, unforgiving harshness of the law. The stone tablets are not nourishing. There is nothing about the stone tablets that would make us want to be near them. Cold. Brutal. Severe. Given to a people that refused to obey.

"For God sent not His son into the world to condemn the world, but that the world through Him might be saved." (John 3:17 KJV)

If we ask for truth, He won't slam us with the stone tablets.

If I am hungry, if I am weak from not eating, if I am reaching for Him, He will not trick us with harshness. He hands us a soft slice of warm, freshly-baked bread. Sometimes He even spreads a generous helping of melted butter on it before He hands it to us.

He Himself is this Bread of Life. To save us *from* deception is why He came! We, His sons and daughters, are invited to the table!

Prayer: Thank you, Lord, for being the Bread from Heaven. Sustain me this day with my daily bread. Lead me not into temptation, but deliver me from evil. Let me not be deceived. Lead me to truth all the days of my life.

Notes

The Word
Became Flesh

John 1:1 (ESV)
"In the beginning was the Word…"

In the sacred space of a Sunday morning, in the hour before I would join the rest of the congregation for Sunday worship, I was praying and pondering.

My mind was on many things. I saw (in my mind) a man walking carefully down the side of a mountain. In his arms he carried the precious, handwritten words of God. I saw another man, sitting on a hillside. His audience was captivated by the words He spoke. Words.

"In the beginning was The Word…" (John 1:1)

"All things were made through Him and without Him was. not. anything. made. that. was. made." (John 1:3 *emphasis mine*)

"He was in the world, and the world was made through Him, yet the world did not know Him." (John 1:10)

"And the Word became flesh and dwelt among us, and we have seen His glory, glory as of the only Son from the Father, full of grace and truth." (John 1:14)

So we need words. We need to articulate truth and structure

through words. Without words is nothing made. Even relationships. Especially discipleship.

Pastors preach. Teachers teach. Evangelists share the gospel—with words. Prophets speak. Apostles use words to inspire.

Words.

Yet He can be spoken, written, and read in the world (among us) and (John 1:10) it can be that the world (us) still doesn't know Him.

In the beginning was the Word. He was somewhere. All things were made by Him. He was busy. At work. Making and shaping. But still, we were unaware. All we had were the impersonal words on distant stone. Rules to live by. Standards to measure up to. Then He became flesh and dwelt among us.

When the Word becomes flesh...

When does the Word become flesh? When we *experience* Him. He becomes flesh when He walks among us. Flesh—the very real, close, touchable, visible, experiential Jesus, walking among us. We see His glory. We know Him. Then, we no longer have a dry word, or legislation, or stone law—a burden to carry.

As Moses came down off the mountain, he carried the stone tablets in both arms. His hands were full. He couldn't use his hands to do anything else. But the man on the hillside said, "I will write my laws in their HEARTS."

This frees up our hands. When the Word becomes flesh and is written in our hearts, our hands are free—to serve. We don't serve because of a list of "words" in a command to do so. Not to stack up a "sufficient" amount of "works." We serve from the overflow.

The man on the hillside stood up. He beckoned to His audience and said clearly, "Come, follow Me. Seek first the Kingdom of God and His righteousness, and all these things shall be added unto you."

I looked at the clock. It was time for me to join the rest of the people that had gathered in the other room to worship and listen. I closed my journal and joined them.

Prayer:

Today, let the prayer come from your heart. Your heart knows.

Notes

_____

_____

_____

_____

_____

_____

_____

_____

_____

_____

_____

_____

How Then
Shall We Trust

Romans 10:14-15 (KJV)
"How then shall they call on Him in whom they have not believed? And how shall they believe in Him of whom they have not heard? And how shall they hear without a preacher? And how shall they preach, except they be sent?"

We believe in Jesus at first when we become born again. After that we believe in Him again and again. It's not only a one-time event, but the first is a picture of the many.

Tonight as I read through these verses, I noticed the words "how then shall they…"

These words, as I read them tonight, sounded like the voice of a reasonable, gentle One. The word believe here is a word that can also be translated as trust. Maybe for the first time ever I saw this passage not as a shameful admonition of not having measured up, but as a compassionate question of encouragement.

He understands trust. He understands that to trust is a process. Sometimes the process is longer and more complicated than at other times. One person can easily trust God for a thing, and this same person can have a very hard time trusting Him for another thing. Jesus understands each part of our process to reach trust.

His compassion amazes me! He has compassion for us at each place where we struggle. Initially when we first believe, we take a step of faith, and it is by faith that we take every step that we take after that. At each point in our lives where we reach yet another hurdle to cross, another area to trust Him in, we can rest assured that He understands. We don't become more trusting when we're getting beat up. Not even when it's ourself who is doing the beating.

"Faith comes by hearing." (Romans 10:17) Want more? Read more. Read scripture out loud to yourself. Our mind is more than our intellect. Our brain has the right side and the left side and our minds are connected with our whole body. We can read scripture, and we can experience more of it when we read it out loud. But be kind to yourself. You learn to trust when a thing or a person is trust*worthy*. Jesus is trustworthy, but we can stand in our own way if we're mean.

How shall they call upon Him in whom they have not believed? Initially for salvation, yes, but also at each crossroad we face. We are our own preacher. We can talk to ourselves as expertly as the best of them. When we saturate our minds with the Word of God, we have the food to feed our soul and it is with our soul that we trust.

The Lord, full of compassion, asks us, "How can you trust Me when you don't believe Me, and how can you believe Me when you haven't heard Me—when your soul hasn't heard Me? And how can you hear Me when you don't let yourself be told? When you don't fill your soul, your mind, and your heart with My Word?"

His Word has been sent. We have it. In kindness to ourselves, we fill our minds with it. A mind full of His Word believes. A person who believes calls on the One they believe in. Every time.

Prayer: Lord, right now I come out of agreement with shame. I apologize to myself for participating in heaping shame on me when I have small faith. I commit right here to disagree with shame and commit to receiving faith Your way. Remind me today if I forget this. Help me be kind to myself and join You in tenderly leading me to a greater trust.

Notes

_____

_____

_____

_____

_____

_____

_____

_____

_____

_____

_____

_____

_____

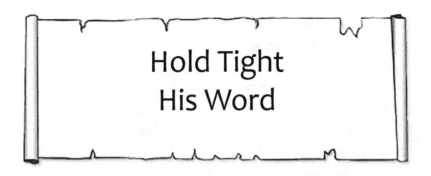

Hold Tight
His Word

Numbers 23:19 (KJV)
"God is not a man, that He should lie. Neither the son of man, that He should repent. Hath He said and shall He not do it? Or hath He spoken and shall He not make it good?"

What has the Lord promised you? What word has He spoken to you? I'm not referring to our wishes or our own imagining. Or things that we would *like* Him to do. What has He spoken when He spoke a definite word to you? That time when you were moved by the firm assurance of His word—to you.

When I was growing up there were people around me who thought it was great fun to play tricks on people. To tease. To use their power to confound the less strong ones. They seemed to believe it was ok to take this trickery all the way to mockery. It left a mark on me. I trusted nothing. Questioned everything. In those days I felt like much of life was a cruel joke.

Perhaps woven into your story are places that have left their mark on you. We have an enemy. His goal is to steal and destroy. He often uses people to accomplish his goal. Man has often been the conduit of harm inflicted on others.

God is not a man that He should lie. When God says a thing, you can take it to the bank! Shall He not make good on His promise? Yes. Yes, He shall! Hold on to the words He has spoken to your heart. Do not let go. No matter what. Take His promise all the way *through* your trial to the end of it. Do not let go of it.

Prayer: Lord, strengthen my mind and my heart to hear, retain, and hold you word. Make me solid and sustain me with strength in my bones. Anoint my head with oil. Put nourishment in my cup today. Make goodness and mercy follow me all the days of my life.

Notes

Be Not Silent
to Me

Psalm 28:1 (KJV)

"Unto Thee will I cry, O Lord my rock; be not silent to me: lest, if Thou be silent to me, I become like them that go down into the pit."

I have found many prayers throughout the Psalms. During some of the hardest times of my life, these prayers seemed to echo the deep, unspeakable cries of my heart.

The same idea with different wording is repeated in Psalm 143:7-8 "Hear me speedily, O Lord! My spirit faileth." (KJV)

Gentle Warrior, have you also felt like you were slipping away into a pit if something doesn't change? Verse 8—"Cause me to hear Thy loving kindness in the morning; for in Thee do I trust." Praying the Word has a whole other dimension of authority. These words are straight from the Holy Spirit. I wish I would have documented every single time that my heart reached that desperate place and I prayed these words from Psalm 28. The Lord met me. Every. Single. Time. I didn't challenge the Lord lightly. I didn't play this card, so to speak, until I needed it. You know the times. You've been there. There aren't words to describe the brokenness we feel when our loved one breaks us. There aren't words. Yet, the Holy Spirit brings the right prayer when we don't know how—or can't—pray.

"*Cause me* to know the way wherein I should walk; for I lift my soul unto Thee.

Deliver me, O Lord, from mine enemies: I flee unto Thee to hide me.

Teach me to do Thy will; for Thou art my God: Thy Spirit is good.

Lead me into the land of uprightness.

Quicken me, O Lord, for Thy name's sake: for Thy righteousness' sake bring my soul out of trouble." ~Psalms 143:8b–11. (KJV)

The King James word 'quicken' is the Hebrew word chayah and it means to restore to life, nourish up, revive, be whole. We can no sooner make ourselves whole in our own power than, without food, a starving human being can strengthen himself. Hide not Thy face from me. Cause me to hear. If You don't speak to me, I'm going down!

The study of the brain, mirror neurons, and why we need face-to-face connection to be healthy is for another time and another book, but Cupcake, we are created by God to need this. It's not a weakness. It's the vein we draw strength from. As the body needs proteins, carbs, and fats to build muscle and bone, so we need the direct words and face-to-face interaction with God to build our soul and our spirit. We're not meant to be alone. When Jesus' time on earth was nearing an end, He promised He wouldn't leave unless He sent Someone. (John 14:25-27)

He knows.

Take a moment and let the Word of God be your prayer today. Take in His Presence. Breathe it in. Reach for it, touch it. Eat it. It's the chayah that will bring you through.

∽

Prayer: Lord, unto You will I cry. You are my Rock. Hide not Your face. Be not silent to me, lest I be like them that go down into the pit! I reach out to You for nourishment. Revive me and I will be whole.

Notes

Psalm 91

Psalm 91:1 (KJV)
"He that dwelleth in the **secret** place of the Most High shall abide under the shadow of the Almighty."

What day and year is today? Today's story is from Psalm 91. Keep today's date in mind and fill in the blanks as you slowly read through it like it was handwritten, by God, personally to you.

If I, today _____, dwell in the secret place of the Most High, I shall abide under the shadow of the Almighty. I will say of the Lord, He is my refuge today _____, and my fortress: My God; in Him will I trust.

He shall cover me today _____ with His feathers, and under His wings shall I trust. His truth shall be my shield and buckler.

I shall not be afraid with terror tonight _____; nor for the arrow that flies by day. Nor for the pestilence that walketh in darkness tonight; nor for the destruction that wasteth tomorrow, _____.

If a thousand shall fall at my side today _____, and ten thousand at my right hand; it shall not come near me.

Only with my eyes shall I behold and see the reward of the

wicked. Because I have made the Lord, which is my refuge, even the Most High, my habitation today _____.

There shall no evil befall me today _____, neither shall any plague come near my dwelling; for He shall give His angels charge over me, to keep my in all my ways. They shall bear me up in their hands, lest I dash my foot against a stone.

Today on _____ I will call upon Him, and He will answer me. He will be with me in trouble. He will deliver me, and honor me. With long life will He satisfy me, and show me His salvation, because I have set my love upon Him.

The broth that is simmered from this Psalm is one that you may want to revisit many times. It never sours. It never loses its strength. It's always there to draw from. Feel free to dip your cup in this broth for as many days as you need it.

Notes

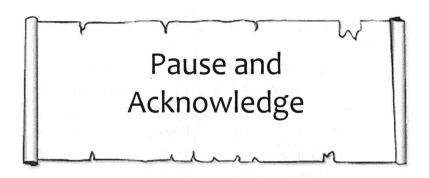

Pause and Acknowledge

Proverbs 3:6 (KJV)
"In all thy ways acknowledge Him and He shall direct thy paths."

The group that gathered around for the meeting were my friends. We went to church together and we were the leaders of all the different departments of our church. The meeting was our bi-monthly meeting, lively, interesting, and provided to us as a way of staying connected and informed. Someone mentioned the proverb in chapter 3, "Trust in the Lord with all thine heart; and lean not unto thine own understanding. In all thy ways acknowledge Him and He shall direct thy paths."

I spoke up. "I've always hated that verse!"

The group erupted in laughter and someone asked me if I'd like to say how I *really* feel.

Realizing how it must have sounded, I recovered with, "No, listen! I *did* always hate that verse for many years! Until recently! It gets quoted *way* too often and too flippantly. It's the band-aid verse that gets slapped onto every crossroad dilemma a poor, unsuspecting person happens to share out loud. But recently I was sitting on my couch, pondering different things and I felt the Lord gently ask me, 'What does acknowledge mean?'"

I asked the group what they thought acknowledge means. They gave me an interesting array of definitions, and I told them what I had thought of that day on the couch. If I acknowledge someone, I might *look* at them. I might step aside to make room for them to pass. If I see someone in a grocery aisle, I might smile and nod. I might give honor to their existence.

What are some ways you might acknowledge someone? This question from the Lord was very eye-opening to me. He is always with us. It takes but a moment to pause and acknowledge a person. Acknowledging is less likely to mean having a long and labored conversation with them, but more likely a quick eye contact, a gesture of aware respect.

My friends at the meeting reacted much the same as I did on the couch that day. I had slowly thought through the familiar verses. "Trust in the Lord with all thine heart; and lean not unto thine own understanding. In all thy ways acknowledge Him and He shall direct thy paths."

The Proverbs are known to pack a punch in a short sentence, and here again is a great secret packed into a few sentences.

Awareness. A turning to look at. A quick connection. A linking of spirit. Here lies the secret of having the Lord get involved in your decisions, your success, your destiny.

In all your ways. A constant awareness.

Keep a respectful awareness of His presence and watch how eager He is to assist you in all your ways.

Prayer: Let not mercy and truth forsake me, Lord. Put them around my neck like a holy necklace. Write them upon the table of my heart. So shall I find favor and good understanding in the sight of God and man. I trust in You, God, with all my heart. I choose today not to lean on my own understanding. I turn my head to see You. Thank you for never leaving my side. I invite you to get involved in all my decisions and definitely my destiny!

(Based on Proverbs 3:3-6)

Notes

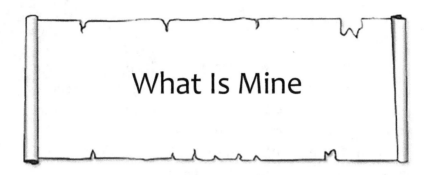

What Is Mine

Psalm 37:5 (NLT)
"Commit everything you do to the Lord, trust Him, and He will help you."

Jewish culture, back in the day, had a custom of sitting in sackcloth and ashes when they were particularly troubled or sorrowful. 2009 was a season of ashes for me. With much crying, I lived in a one-day-at-a-time mode that year.

One particular morning I made my cup of coffee and decided to sit with God until a ray of light broke through. The Lord led me through a series of Bible passages and we ended up in Psalm 37. In this year when the proverbial "sackcloth" was suffocating me and the "ashes" made such a cloud of darkness around me that I couldn't see the future, the Lord slowly and deliberately took me, phrase by phrase, through the first nine verses of Psalm 37.

"Don't worry about the wicked."

"Don't envy those who do wrong."

"Trust in the Lord, and do good."

We often read too fast. We think fast, we live fast, and we quickly grab a bite from the Word of God as we rush out the door to live our busy lives.

"Trust in the Lord."

"Do good."

Here are six short words that we can live by. Six phrases to "simmer" all day long in our crock pot of meditations. Six ethics to make decisions by. Six whispers to hush the turmoil in the mind. Six points to focus on throughout the day.

In the first nine little verses of Psalm 37, there are a list of imperatives and a balancing list of what God will do. His part is His to worry about. We can only do what's ours to do. We can't do our part AND His part. That's too much for us. A large part of the chaos in my life that year I could do nothing about. When this is the case, we can shut out the growling hiss of the maelstrom and focus on the thing that we *can do*.

"Take delight in the Lord."

"Commit everything you do to the Lord."

"Trust Him."

"Be still in the presence of the Lord."

"Wait patiently for Him to act."

"Don't worry about evil people." This one alone lifted a heavy load off of my mind. The Lord would later ask me to stand and confront some evil, but not this day. Not in the day of sackcloth. Not in the day when the ashes burned my eyes. This day He asked me not to worry about evil people. We can't even see straight when we're in this condition, much less make good judgment calls. When we release our minds from worry, it's easier to do the next thing in this inspired list: "stop your anger."

The last of my coffee had long grown cold as I slowly absorbed the strength the Lord was offering to me that day. "Don't worry about evil people." The way He spoke it to my heart that day was not in the casual brush of a hand as we would brush away a few unwanted crumbs. He spoke it in a way that communicated to my crushed heart that it's HIS part to worry about them. Someone needed to. The evil in the world—in my world—needed to be brought to justice. But on this day, when I couldn't, He could.

He speaks tenderly. His words communicate depth. And value. He knows what we need and as I felt the strength of His care seep into me, I did see a glimmer of light. The coffee left in my cup might have been cold, but His love was warm. And the light was a welcome sense.

Trust in the Lord.

Do good.

Prayer: Lord, when my heart is too heavy to do good, you are able to lift my load. Show me today what I'm carrying that isn't mine to carry. Show me what *is* mine.

"The salvation of the righteous is of the Lord. He is their strength in the time of trouble. And the Lord shall help them, and deliver them: He shall deliver them from the wicked, and save them, because they trust Him" (Psalm 37:38-39 KJV).

Notes

_____

_____

_____

_____

_____

_____

Key of Trust

1 Chronicles 5:20 (NET)
"They received divine help in fighting them, and the Hagarites and all their allies were handed over to them. They cried out to God during the battle; He responded to their prayers because they trusted Him."

In the middle of a gruesome story of war in the Old Testament, like an archaeologist, I unearthed a key. Trust.

These were bloody men of war. Not the average 2020 American Christians. Not the well-behaved godly men from the National Pastor's Association. They were ruffians and warriors. I can imagine they had the Hebrew vocabulary equal to a sailor. But the Lord wants us to know that during the battle, He responded to their prayers *because they trusted Him.*

We have an accuser that whispers to us that because we have sinned or because we currently haven't yet overcome the battle we face, that God couldn't possibly WANT to hear our prayer because we are failing Him. Sometimes the enemy stands before us, shouting at us, "God can't hear you!!"

Why is our enemy so committed in delivering these lies to us? Because he wants us to give up!

Trust is key here in our battle. Sometimes it helps to picture what we're reading. Imagine with me for a moment that trust has an aroma. God is always near. He will never forsake us, but picture a scenario with me and let's imagine that we can follow trust to see where it goes and how it plays out. Let's say God is in Heaven, on His throne, listening to Angel music, and thinking thoughts that only God can think.

All of a sudden He says, "Angels! Hush! I smell something! I love that scent! It smells like . . . trust! Where's it coming from?"

A messenger angel steps forward and says, "Sir, the aroma is coming from (fill in your name here_____) (Anna Noa Grace), the gentle warrior from (_____your region.)

He stands majestically up from His throne and says, "Let's go see! I will visit this trusting soldier today and they will win because of Me!"

See, the Principalities (mentioned in Ephesians 6) can't trust. They also can't absorb the aroma of trust, to prevent it from getting through. The essence of trust floats past every layer of power mentioned in Ephesians, right on up, all the way to the throne.

We can trust God based on HIS merit, not ours. Obviously we want to live in obedience. The verse that says, "be holy as I am holy" is still a valid verse, but while we're still in whatever state we are, we can realize that life is a journey. Holiness is a journey and not a destination. We don't have to measure up to a certain level of maturity in order to trust God in the battle. HE is trustworthy and we can trust Him. He stands and takes notice of the trusting one no matter *where* the trusting one is. Like the rugged soldiers in war a thousand years before Christ, we too, can cry out to God and pledge our trust in Him.

Take heart, Tender One, pick up your head. The battle is not over, but God is on our side. Go directly against the suggestion of the enemy and fully trust God, even foolishly trust God. God is attracted to the scent of trust.

For today's prayer time I present to you Psalm 31. Scan through the whole chapter and form a prayer right out of the words of King David. Praying the Word is as powerful as Isaiah 55:11 says it is! Be strong, Soldier! We win in the end. If we haven't yet won, it's not yet the end.

Notes

Reacting or Responding

Proverbs 26:4 (KJV)
"Answer not a fool according to his folly, lest thou also be like unto him."

One of my goals in life is to reach a place where I do not react, only respond. Reacting is the dialect of the victim. Ironically, a victim is often unaware that he speaks victim. As prisoners, we're partly held captive by our own behaviors and have to learn to detect our own dialect.

Verse 5 of the same chapter in Proverbs says, "Answer a fool according to his folly, lest he be wise in his own conceit."

These two verses could be seen as rough-hewn blocks of un-polished bookends on a whole shelf of books full of experience and training. To know when to keep silent and when to speak and what to say if we do speak cannot be learned in one afternoon. In our journey out of victimhood we begin to learn that our response is our choice, and as we learn, we can begin to speak with a new accent.

How I respond is my choice. As I develop my relationship with God, and let Him put into my heart the love that I need, I can respond to those around me. I believe this is a primary visual of the fruit of the Spirit called self-control.

Imagine the tumultuous catfight of two fools trying to accomplish verse five! Treasured One, one of us needs not to be a fool. In James 1:5 we find a rich cup of broth to sip on for days . . . "If any of you need wisdom, you should ask God, and it will be given to you. God is generous and won't correct you for asking." (CEV) I love this verse. If we lack wisdom, we won't acquire it by beating ourselves up. It simply says, "ask God and it will be given." The enemy of our soul would like to keep us ignorant. Be aware of this. This journey towards wellness and wholeness won't be without a fight. Don't give up when you don't feel wise as soon as you've asked. We are His favorite. He delights in giving us what we ask for and need. He feeds us wisdom—one cup at a time.

Between Proverbs 26:4 and 5, dive into the experience! Learn all that you can and fill your own books with as much exciting adventure as God designed for you. He calls, He waits, He delights to take you on this amazing journey toward wisdom and freedom.

Prayer:

In John 1:1, it says that You are the Word. Come and fill me today. Put Your word in my heart that I might not sin against You, that I might not sin against myself, that I might not sin against my loved one. You are the Word. Fill me with You. Make me aware of my own accent and teach me to speak in the dialect of Your Kingdom.

Notes

Hear My Voice

John 10:27-28 (KJV)

"My sheep hear my voice, and I know them, and they follow me. And I give unto them eternal life; and they shall never perish, neither shall any man pluck them out of my hand."

The King James version says no one can "pluck" them. Several other versions say "snatch." I got curious and looked this word up in the Greek. It is "harpazo" and has the meaning of being seized by force, pulled, or taken.

Adversity in this life is pretty much a given. We all have hardships and sometimes our troubles reach unbearable levels. In the trouble I've had, I have felt this pull. Sometimes it feels like I'm being sucked under. Sometimes it feels like I'm being "shoved out," out over the edge. Sometimes it feels like suffocation. In any case, this "harpazo" word for the kidnapping of our soul would apply.

God's plan is to keep you in His hand and the enemy's plan is to pull you away. Jesus said that no one *can* pluck you out of God's hand, but that doesn't mean no one *tries!* In this short story in John 10, as soon as Jesus had said these things, the people around Him picked up actual stones to throw at Him—to stone Him to death. I have found that a similar scenario happens in our lives. Everything we gain gets tested. And there will always be people who "throw stones."

Jesus gives us the essential key in this conflict or outright war—cultivate your ability to hear His voice. "My sheep hear My voice, and I know them, and they follow Me." When you're right in the gory center of a trial, it can get pretty hard to discern His voice. There can be so *many* voices clamoring at us when things are thick. But we *must* hear Him.

We can develop an ear in the middle of a crisis, but it helps to have had practice before the attack comes. We all have twenty-four hours in a day. I'd rather see us use our time getting so used to hearing His voice, that when the bad time comes we have an ear to hear.

Education is great. Experience and counsel are wonderful. We can gather a lot of data and build support groups, which are essential to the human wellbeing, but when it comes down to it, only His voice can get us through to victory. In an all-out test of our faith, the relationship will get us through.

Prayer: Oh Lord, let me never, ever be deceived. Train me to hear and to hear well. I want to follow You and walk with You wherever You lead. Protect my soul from damage. Let me be sensitive to Your whispered word. Make Your voice plain to me that I not miss what You're saying.

Notes

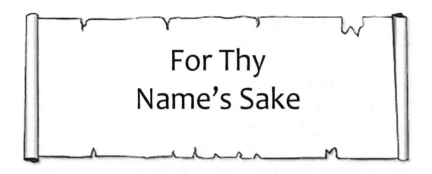

For Thy Name's Sake

Psalm 79:9 (KJV)
"Help us, Oh God of our salvation, for the glory of thy name: and deliver us, and purge away our sins, for Thy name's sake."

One chilly, crispy morning as I sat wrapped up in a fuzzy blanket, studying the Psalms and praying for my family, I began to see a theme.

I had been praying for years and even saw many answers to my prayers, but this day I began to see the theme of "for the glory of Thy name." I pondered a long time on what I had been praying and on what I might begin praying.

"For Thy name's sake."

There are times that I have gotten wrapped up in my own saga and neglected to see the Grand Saga. What is happening in my life? What is happening in my life in regard to the story of the whole Creation and life as God planned it? Am I wanting answers to prayers so that my life is more comfortable and pleasing? Am I wanting prayers answered for His name's sake?

The whole story is His story—from the beginning. In the beginning God . . . We own a small part of the story that is ours to live, but the Greater Story began with God, will continue with God, and will end how He writes it. When we as God's people fail, the real question is not "did I hurt my reputation," but more importantly, the question is "how is my life reflecting His name?"

I began that day to pay attention to my prayers. Why do I want my husband saved? Why do I want our marriage to overcome and thrive? So that we look successful? Yes and no. Mostly no. I want to reflect His name well. We don't live alone on an island. We're surrounded by both believers and unbelievers. I don't want God's name trashed. God doesn't want His name trashed.

"Deliver us and purge away our sins, for Thy name's sake."

If we wanna get our prayers answered, let's join God in His story.

Prayer: Psalm 115:1–2 (NKJV) "Not to us, O Jehovah, not to us, but unto Your name give glory, for Your mercy, and for Your truth's sake. Wherefore should the nations say, 'Where now is their God?'" Lord, make Your name great in me today. Make me to walk in ways that reflect Your character well. If the heathen around me are asking where my God is, I pray that You will come strong on my behalf and not let them wonder long. Prove Your presence for Your name's sake!

Notes

Twelve Dusty Stones

Joshua 4:5b-7 (NIV)
"Each of you is to take up a stone on his shoulder, according to the number of the tribes of the Israelites, to serve as a sign among you. In the future when your children ask you, 'What do these stones mean?' tell them...when [we] crossed the Jordan, the waters of the Jordan were cut off."

Yesterday my pastor used the story in Joshua 4 and 5 to encourage us to follow the Lord in the new things into which He is leading us. Joshua is an interesting read. If you haven't read it recently, I would like to invite you to a banquet of encouragement in the book of Joshua.

God had already done a host of miracles for His people by the time they got to the Jordan and were getting prepared for the final piece of their journey into the Promised Land. As they cross the Jordan in yet *another* outrageous miracle—crossing it on dry ground—the Lord instructed them to choose twelve men and assign to them the job of carrying twelve stones out of the middle of the river bed. They were to take them along to the Promised Land. For a memorial. A constant, solid reminder of who God is and what He can do.

My mind has a crazy sense of the visual. When my pastor read the words "carry the stones on their shoulders..." I saw them. I saw the stones. I saw the dust falling off the stones. I saw the sweaty faces of the men as they were carrying the heavy stones out. The Bible doesn't say how large the stones were, but in my imagination I saw them as large and heavy.

The idea of carrying something on your shoulder made me think of the idiom we say when someone has a "chip on his shoulder."

I hope no one from the congregation was analyzing my face just then, because I have no idea what they would have found there. I was in another zone, watching a whole new scene unfold in my mind. I imagined my big, burly men carrying the portly, dusty rocks through the Jordan river bed, and I imagined the man in the 20th century, in a small crowd of his friends with a chip on his shoulder.

For one, the size difference was remarkable. The large, significant boulder of remembrance of what God had done compared to the tiny, jagged chip almost made me giggle. Metaphorically though, I was very sobered. I imagined carrying the testimony of what God has done for *me*. Remembering what God has done and who He is is not a heavy load of weight, but it is weighty in importance—a constant awareness of why we can trust. I can't hold a grudge in my hands if I'm busy holding a rock of remembrance of the goodness of my Savior.

I imagined the difference in impact. If I carry—in obvious sight—the testimony of His power and I'm around other people, they will see and know the God I serve. If I carry an abrasive chip on my shoulder around other people, they will see and know that, too. I mean, just imagine the difference. The chip represents an injustice *done* to me *or* my desire to exact judgment on others. (You want to harm me? Huh! I'll show you! You see this chip on my shoulder?) I mean, really! What a ridiculous way to threaten people. Like a chip will really be a viable weapon against the enemy.

The Israelites didn't bring chips on their shoulders against Jericho. They brought the powerful, effective Word of the Lord. They heard. They obeyed. They walked it out. They carried the stones of testimony and defeated their foes, not themselves.

Prayer: Lord, today as I sit to ponder, I ask that you train my mind to hold the goodness, the miraculous, the wonder of You and carry that. I ask that you train me to melt away the need to judge or count grievances. You are well able to take care of me. Teach me to walk tall and carry Your goodness well.

Notes

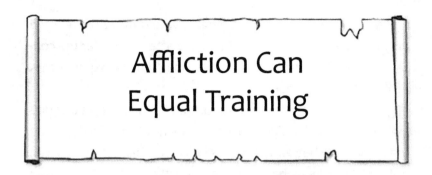

Affliction Can Equal Training

Psalm 119:67 (KJV)
"Before I was afflicted I went astray: but now I have kept Your word."

God is doing something in you whether you see it right now or not.

Affliction. I think of training an animal like a horse, a mule, a camel, or a sled dog. Untrained, these animals are nearly useless. They have value, they have a place on earth, but they don't contribute and don't carry much profit in the marketplace. Training might feel like negative affliction, but once an animal is trained, however, they don't just require money, leaching off the owner, but they contribute value and a service in return for the care they receive.

The Psalmist writes, "Before I was afflicted, I went astray."

In my own life I have often felt that weight of choice being presented to me. In affliction we can choose what to do with it. We can't always choose what happens in life, but when it does happen, there may be some things He wants to do *in* you before He does something *with* you.

We feel frustration in training. It would make sense if we only had to suffer for our own sins but often we suffer the consequences of our broken world. The affliction we experience is often unfair and ungodly.

I have heard good people say to the afflicted one, "Suffering makes us better." I highly disagree. It's not the suffering itself that makes us better. It's what choice we make IN it that can potentially make us better. If we use affliction as an organized opportunity to dive deep into all things God, we can indeed become better for having gone through the trial.

"May I wholeheartedly follow Your decrees, that I may not be put to shame." (Psalm 119:80 NIV)

"If Your law had not been my delight, I would have perished in my affliction. (Psalm 119:92 NIV)

The choice presented to us is right there. Will we let God train us, or will we let evil kill us? Will we fight the affliction for the sake of getting rid of it, or will we let it be the engine that drives us into God?

An untrained horse has a lot of power to resist, but what value does it bring to the world?

"I am Thine. Save me for I have sought Thy precepts." (Psalm 119:94 KJV)

Prayer: Lord, clean my heart of selfish ambitions, of small mindedness. Teach me Your ways. Teach me as I wait and use this time to soak deep into the Word. Open my eyes to the deeper things that You want to teach me as I go through this trial. Let me see things Your way.

Notes

Set a Watch

Psalm 141:3 (KJV)
"Set a watch, O Lord, before my mouth; keep the door of my lips."

Again, no matter what gets thrown at us, are we willing to let adversity motivate us to become a better person? Returning evil for evil is for the fool. To "set a watch" does not mean we say nothing—a cold-shouldered silent treatment. Evil flourishes when good men do nothing. To "keep the door" doesn't mean we nail it shut.

A watchman and keeper are busy doing something. It's an active role. A doorkeeper is in charge of letting authorized personnel in and out. When we ask the Lord to set a watch, we participate with Him to give conscious thought to what we say.

"Let your gentleness be evident to all. The Lord is near." (Philippians 4:5 NIV) The Lord is near. He is as near as the breath we take. He's always available. A study of Philippians 4:5 to 9 would be a good side dish to add to today's cup of nourishment.

I encourage you to keep on asking for wisdom. I have found

that when I ask the Lord, He brings to my attention the harmful things I let in and out of my doors.

The Lord is gentle and He is near. He is able to gently remind you when you are about to say something foolish. The same goes for what comes into our doors. We are what we think. Set a guard on your thoughts. Take charge of your thoughts. Your thoughts are not in charge of you. You are in charge of them.

We might be surrounded by people who do not practice this watchmanship. We might be called to speak up. With Jesus stationed at our door, we have a wise doorkeeper who will hold the light of truth as He guards our hearts and minds.

Prayer: "Let not my heart be drawn to what is evil, to take part in wicket deeds with men who are evildoers; let me not eat their delicacies." (Psalm 141:4 NIV) Lord, be the doorkeeper of my mouth. Make me aware of what goes in and out. Let me speak words that are good and approved by You. Show me when to keep silent and when to speak. I need Your peace to keep my mind and my heart safe from unruly explosions. Let me be gentle and exhibit Your character, even when You ask me to speak up.

Notes

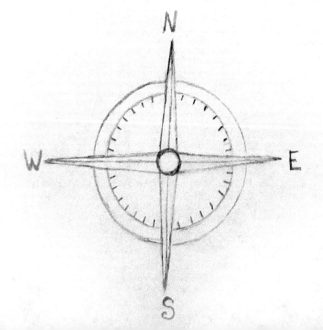

Turn and
Be Filled

Proverbs 1:23 (KJV)
"Turn you at my reproof: Behold I will pour out my Spirit unto you, I will make known my words unto you."

I study many translations. Someday I'd like to study Hebrew. For now I rely on Hebrew dictionaries and various translations. I notice that the New International Version put this verse in past tense. (If you had responded...I would have poured.) All my other translations put the verse in present tense. An imperative.

I'm so thankful that our chance to submit to God is not over!

Here's an interesting question to ask ourselves. How do we feel when God reproves us? Sometimes it makes me angry. Sometimes I'm willing to agree with Him right away. And sometimes I'm mature enough to be grateful for His reproof.

Life on earth is hard. It's harder when we're stupid, right? I don't know who "they" are in Prov. 1:30-31. I hope to God that it's not me! It says, "They would [have] none of my counsel. They despised all my reproof. Therefore shall they eat the fruit of their own way, and be filled with their own devices." I don't know about you, but I would rather have His Spirit poured on me and His words made known to me than to eat the fruit of my own way.

There is a first part and a second part of our verse today. The second is second for a reason. The New Living Translation says, "Come here and listen to me!" Regardless of how we might feel at each corrective reprimand from God, we first have to turn TO Him before we can expect to have His Spirit poured, and our cup filled with wisdom.

When we're in a hard place, we do better to check our "compass" than to place blame. Am I turned my own way or am I turned in a posture of receiving instruction from the Lord? We're not promised an easy, trouble-free life. The Christian will be tested. There's no way around it. The Word of God tells us this. But the verse today is talking about the essentials we need to navigate successfully. We *need* His Spirit and we *need* wisdom. These are not poured unconditionally like His love is. It says, "Behold, I *will* pour." (Look, I will do this for you, but you need to turn to me.)

This "turning" happens daily. We don't turn once and then we're done with turning. We turn back to God as many times as we drift our own way. Each day. Each crisis. Each argument. Each project. Each conflict with a spouse. Each confrontation with our child. All day long we're given the choice to go our own way or turn to God for wisdom.

Thank God!! Thank God that this opportunity to receive His reproof is open to us!

Prayer: Dear God, thank You for Your reproof. Thank You for your instruction. Thank You for each chastisement. Thank You that You love me enough to correct me when I'm wrong. Thank You that You save me, even from my own way. I hold my heart in my hand and lift it up to You for a full pouring. Pour Your Spirit into me and fill me with Your wisdom!

Notes

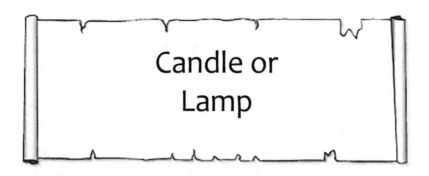

Candle or Lamp

Leviticus 24:2 (MKJV)
"Command the sons of Israel that they bring to you pure olive oil, beaten, for the light, to cause the lamps to burn continually."

Throughout Exodus and Leviticus we can read about the careful instructions God gave to Moses to make the tabernacle after the pattern which he was shown on the mountain. A study of the tabernacle is quite fascinating. Every part of it has a spiritual meaning.

It occurred to me one day that lamp and candle were used interchangeably in these instructions. I looked it up. Was it a candle or was it a lamp? I found that the word candlestick is used to describe the artistic stand these lamps were on. The light itself was a lamp that burned oil. They weren't burning the 20th century candles that we have today - made from beeswax, soybean, or synthetic materials. These lamps on fancy candlesticks were lamps fueled by oil.

So what? Who cares? But ponder this: A candle consumes itself. An oil lamp burns and gets its power *from the oil*.

"Thy Word is a lamp unto my feet and a light unto my path." (Psalm 119:105 KJV)

Another specific instruction, given to the priests, was to tend these lamps every morning and every evening. Clearly we need to tend our lamps—always, but when we're hit hard by opposition or crisis we for sure need Light to walk by! You know those days! (Sometimes weeks and months!) We feel drained and exhausted and so very tired of the battle.

If "Thy Word" is my "lamp" and I need to "tend" it, I was wondering what "Thy Word" meant, because whoever wrote this Psalm wouldn't have had the Bible as we know it today. I looked that up too. It's the Hebrew word dabar and it would take a page to list all the meanings of it! It means everything from speech, to business, to judgment, to promise, to word, and more! The list of words I found to describe dabar sound like an interaction of communication. Living. Alive. Current.

Thy Word is a lamp. Ok. And this lamp needs fuel. Israel was commanded, "You go get the oil. You bring it." To me this is action-packed. Our relationship with our Lord is interactive. We are active participants. We sit, we study, we search, we speak, we clear space, we invite, we wait, He speaks, we get up, we walk, we watch, we gather, we come back, we bring what we found that day, we sit, we ponder, He talks, we listen, we savor His words to us. They're not just words. We've "done business" with Him. He smiles. We know it. We feel it. It empowers us.

We, in our own strength, will wear out, get tired, and consume ourselves. But if we are filled with power, the oil, the Holy Spirit, we keep walking and living in the Light.

Prayer time: Your space with the Lord is so sacred that I hesitate to enter it with you today. I invite you to clear space, sit, speak, and wait. If He directs you to dig into the written word, go there. If He directs you to study the meanings within a verse, go there. But bring it. Bring your hunger and do the activity you sense He asks of you. Let today's time with Him be personally yours and His.

Notes

Fasting

Isaiah 58:9 (KJV)
"Then shalt thou call, and the Lord shall answer; thou shalt cry, and He shall say, 'Here I am.' If thou take away from the midst of thee, the yoke, the putting forth of the finger, and speaking vanity."

"Is this not the fast I have chosen?" Isaiah 58:5 (To supplement today's devotion, I recommend reading the whole chapter of Isaiah 58.)

Much has been written about the merits of fasting. I have personally found it to be a powerful resource. If God asks me to fast, I can fast as many days as He wants and stay strong in physical strength through it. If it's not a fast called by God, my body can't handle it very well. But that's me. Each of us has to seek His face and ask Him when, and for how long, He wants us to fast.

One of the great benefits of fasting is that it clears our heads and tunes our spirit into God's Spirit. It is a sacred time of covenant between yourself and God, and should be treated as such. According to Isaiah 58, there is definitely a right way and a wrong way to fast. We shouldn't "sit in sackcloth and ashes" when we fast to try to get God to feel sorry for us. Or even to stir up a sense of pity for ourselves, crying because we don't get to eat food. Believe me—plenty of "feelings" come up when you subject yourself to a fast! You will feel all kinds of emotions! This is okay. Let them come, and let them pass. Fasting is the time when you clear out a lot of rubbish!

The Lord says, "Then shall we call, and the Lord shall answer; we shall cry, and He shall say, 'Here I am.' If we take away the yoke, the putting forth of the finger, and speaking vanity." In a fast, ask yourself if you're putting any undue pressure on yourself, or on others. Take the "yoke" off during a fast. Release yourself from the ever-present score card, and for the duration of the fast, don't keep score on the ones around you.

In releasing yourself from oppression, you might need to "vent" to God and tell Him the trouble others have been, but when you're done with that, take the finger you pointed at others and lay it in your lap. Don't corrode your sacred fast with a lot of finger-pointing. Let it rest. And our mouth! Oh, our mouth! What vanity we speak! The King James Version calls it vanity. The New International calls it malicious talk. The New Living says vicious rumors. In a fast, we shut down the tongue, and especially so if we are caught in a web of gossip and slander. It seems that in a fast, our words are weighed on a very keen scale.

If we can do these three things in a fast—lift the yoke, stop pointing the finger, speak no vain thing—then we are well on our way to a breakthrough! Then we shall call, and the Lord shall answer. "Here I am" are wonderful words when the Lord is saying them personally to us.

If you're in an especially tough spot now, or find yourself in one in the future, maybe it's time to bring out the big guns and go on a fast. Check with the Lord and be smart about it. Drink lots of water. Grape juice or a mild, low sugar juice can be good for your body. My prayer for each of you is that you reach an incredible breakthrough when you do fast!

Notes

Made Perfect

1 John 4:16 (KJV)
"God is love; and he that dwelleth in love dwelleth in God, and God in him."

Few people wrestle with the concept of perfection like the melancholy Christian. To us, perfection is the tyrant and we its helpless subjects.

One balmy day in summer, I was listening to the Bible on audio as I cleaned my bedroom. No one was bothering me. I had ample liberty for my imagination to glide, dip, and soar along as the British voice read verse after verse to me. The bedroom was beginning to look less like a homeless shelter and more like an inviting chamber of rest when my British friend on audio read 1 John 4 to me.

The voice read verse 18; "There is no fear in love; but perfect love casteth out fear: because fear hath torment. He that feareth is not made perfect in love."

I sat on my bed and played chapter 4 over and over. After years of striving to be good and longing to be perfect, yet never being good enough, and always missing the perfect mark, I was finally seeing what the Lord was showing me! It's IN love. Inside of love.

I got my Bible out and read it. "The Father sent the son to be the Savior of the World. Whosoever shall confess that Jesus is the Son of God, God dwelleth IN him, and he IN God. God is love. He that dwelleth IN love dwelleth IN God, and God IN him. We have boldness in the day of JUDGMENT because as He is, so are we in this world. There is no fear in love. Perfect love casteth out fear, because fear hath torment. He that feareth is. not. made. perfect. IN. love. We love Him, because He first loved us. [1 John 4:14-19 (condensed) KJV, *emphasis mine*]

Ahhh! The rest of the cleaning would just have to wait a moment. I needed time to be fully present with the marvel I just uncovered!

If I am inside of love, I am fully experiencing ... love. Fully experiencing love has no fear. There is no failure. We are confident on judgment day—any day that we're getting judged. Sometimes I myself am my worst judge. *I* cannot make myself perfect! All the effort I would put in throughout an entire lifetime would not make me perfect! Trying harder won't get me anywhere closer to that elusive perfection I seek!

Bringing His love inside of me *is* what cleanses me and shapes me into the image of Him. The more I live in His love, the more I am like Him. The way I had been living was the other way around. I had lived my belief that I needed to *love* more perfectly *so that* I could be more like Him. Or even be acceptable *to* Him. The Father sent the Son to be the Savior of the world. He didn't send me to be the savior of me. There *is* already a perfect Savior! My part is to relax INTO Him and *let* Him be my Savior! He was the Savior. First. We love Him because He first loved us! On the day we first believed, and on this day! And the next. And the day after that.

He didn't save our soul and say, ok, now learn to live well on your own.

Have you experienced the stiffness inside when you are trying really hard to be perfect? The tension? Oh, the tension! I know it well! If love comes close, I would sooner push it away when I don't feel *worthy* of it. Imagine letting all of that go and imagine what it would be like to bring love in! Feel the softening? Feel the tension leaving your shoulders? Breathe! Settle back. *Let* Him be your Savior. He *is*.

Prayer: Oh Lord! Forgive me for my self-centeredness! You and You alone are the Savior of the world! Save me today—from myself! I do choose this moment to invite Your love in. I ask that you melt away the pride and perfectionism in me. Make me new. Make me like You!

Notes

Not to Harm

Jeremiah 29:11 (NIV)
"For I know the plans I have for you, declares the Lord, plans to prosper you and not to harm you, plans to give you hope and a future."

Many times when we're going through an extended period of trials we can be convinced that God is out to harm us. It feels so true in the hard times. It feels like God has left us or at best doesn't give two bits about what we're feeling. In those times we have to talk to ourselves. Faith does, after all, come by hearing (Romans 10:17). What *feels* true may not be what *is* true. Throughout the Psalms we see the writer of Psalms talking to his own soul, telling it what to believe. Encouraging himself to believe God and be strong. Telling his soul to praise God even in the midst of great danger.

The Word of God is true and He tells us that He knows the plans He has for us. He's got plans, folks! And they're plans to prosper you! The King James Version uses the word "thoughts." "I know the thoughts I think towards you." He's thinking of you. And His thoughts are not thoughts of how He'd like to harm you! His thoughts are thoughts of peace. Thoughts of how He'd like to bring you to a place of soundness. A place where your relationships are friendships and your friendships are peaceful.

Don't take the baited hook the enemy throws out to you that God is far off and that He intends to harm you. Not true. God plans to give you hope. Reach for the hope. Believe. Believe against all odds. He's thinking about you, my friend. Thinking and planning on your behalf.

Jeremiah 29:12-14a "When you call out to Me and come and pray to Me, I'll hear you. You will seek Me and find Me when you search for me with all your heart. I'll be found by you, declares the Lord, and I'll restore your security and gather you from [all the places you've gone]." (ISV)

Prayer: (Psalm 27:7-9)*"Hear, O Lord, when I cry aloud; be gracious to me and answer me! You have said, 'seek my face.' My heart says to you, 'Your face, Lord, do I seek.' Hide not your face from me. Turn not your servant away in anger, O You who have been my help. Cast me not off; forsake me not, O God of my salvation!"* I choose to believe that You do have plans for me and that You plan to prosper me and not harm me.

Notes

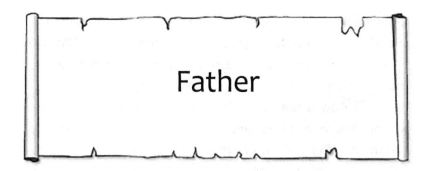

Father

Ephesians 3:14-15 (MKJV)
"For this cause I bow my knees to the Father of our Lord Jesus Christ, of whom the whole family in Heaven and earth is named."

I have a large hardcover book, about two inches thick, called a Concordance. It may be about as obsolete as cassette tapes and vinyl records, but I have one, nonetheless. One sultry August morning I had an idea. A friend of mine wanted our Bible Study group to study fathers and what it means to have God as our Father. The idea that came to me was to open my two-inch-thick antique and look for all the references to father and see where it leads me.

The words in a Concordance are listed alphabetical—like a dictionary. As my eyes scanned down the eleven long columns of the word father, I noticed that there was only one capitalized reference to Father in the entire Old Testament, and in the New Testament, the references were almost all capitalized.

This intrigued me!

I looked up the one capitalized reference in the Old Testament. It was Isaiah 9:6—a prophesy about Jesus. "For to us a Child is born, to us a Son is given; and the government shall be on His shoulder; and His name shall be called Wonderful, Counselor, The mighty God, The everlasting Father, The Prince of Peace." (MKJV)

At that point, my idea just became an invitation from God to come find Him.

While God is the same yesterday, today, and forever, He was not known as *Father* until Jesus. Over and over in the Old Testament I found God referred to as "The Lord God of your fathers." Everything changes when we step from the Old to the New. Jesus came to reveal the nature of God as our Father. In Matthew 4:17, He comes on the scene saying, "Repent for the kingdom of heaven is at hand." (KJV) I looked up the Greek word for "at hand." It means to bring near, to join one thing to another.

When His disciples asked Him to teach them how to pray, He taught them to pray, "Our Father." Through Jesus, He is no longer the distant, fire-and-smoke God of our fathers. He is *my* Father. Jesus came to join one thing to another. To bring us near.

I had a lot to tell my Bible Study group.

The next time we met we had a lively conversation! We explored some of the implications of what this all means. Like Galatians 4:4-7; "When the fullness of the time came, God sent forth His Son, coming into being out of a woman, having come under the law, that He might redeem those under the law, so that we might receive the adoption of sons. And because you are sons, God has sent forth the Spirit of His Son into your hearts, crying Abba Father, so that you are no longer a slave, but a son; and if a son, also an heir of God through Christ." (MKJV)

The deeply profound opportunity to have a relationship with God as our Father is not something to take for granted. Live in it to the fullest, my friend!

Prayer: For this cause I bow my knees to you, Father, of whom I have my name. Thank You with all my heart that You are good and that You are my Father and that I am Yours! Teach me what it means to be an heir through Christ.

"But as many as received Him, to them gave He power to become sons of God, even to them that believe on His name" (John 1:12 KJV).

Notes

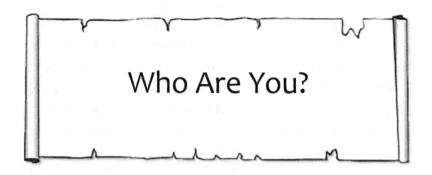

Who Are You?

Philippians 2:5 (KJV)
"Let this mind be in you which was also in Christ Jesus."

How did Jesus think? How did He think of Himself? How am I to think? How am I to think of myself? Let's dip a cup of broth from Phil. 2:6-7 "[Jesus] being in the form of God, thought it not robbery to be equal with God. But made Himself of no reputation and took upon Himself the form of a servant and was made in the likeness of men." (KJV)

During His time here as a man, Jesus often had to encounter opposition that took various forms of the accusation "who do you think you are?" Even in the three tries the devil had with Jesus in the wilderness there was the phrase "if you are…" questioning His identity and demanding of Jesus to *prove* who He was. Can you identify? Have you encountered this spirit lately?

He *is* the Son of God. He's the Son of God whether He pulls rank and privilege or whether He picks up the towel. He chose to serve and God asks me to let this mind be in me. What is this mind?

"It is God which worketh in you both to will and to do of His good pleasure" (Phil. 2:13 KJV). When you get verbal attacks for being a good person and doing good in the world, remember on one hand you have the option of clinging to status, and on the other hand you have behavior because of position. What I see in Philippians is an encouragement to switch from assessing whether others are comprehending our royalty and focus instead on whether we are behaving like the Son/Daughter that we *are*.

The Greek word translated *form* in Phil. 2:6 means to be in the shape, nature, and form of. Jesus, "being in the form of God" had God's shape and *nature*. The Bible says of us that we are made in the image of God also. The question is, do we have His nature? Or do we covet His authority without actually having His nature? He didn't think it was putting on airs to be like God—to behave equal to His nature.

"It is God which worketh in you both to will and to do of His good pleasure." It's an evil spirit that would want to strip a person of their God-given talents and callings! It's also an evil spirit that comes in various forms to blur and skew our identity, trying to remove us from the security of who we are as Sons and Daughters.

God is the ultimate authority. He is the Alpha. He is the King of kings and no one can take His place. AND God's authority is not of the nature that eliminates all other authority or His children's authority. Having ultimate authority, He does not sit there holding it, refusing that any other person or being have ANY. He doesn't hoard and exclude. God's authority makes room and space for His Sons and Daughters to move in the authority He has invested in them.

So to Sons and Daughters, I could say on one hand don't try to prove who you are. On the other hand, just be who you are. There's an ENTIRELY different attitude in the two. One is striving and one is resting. We ARE the Sons, the Daughters. We don't have to grasp at the position or cling to the status. Knowing I am the Daughter, I can behave equal to my position.

Know who you are and be it.

Shape and nature.

Serving and servanthood don't cancel our royalty. Jesus, knowing who he was, took the towel and washed His disciples' feet. (John 13:3-5) If I find myself not behaving like a daughter, I need to go back to God and ask Him to fill me with the Holy Spirit *more*, so that I have His *nature*. Both in authority and in servanthood.

Prayer: Tell me who I am, God. I will believe Your description of me. Let my mind be so filled with You that my mind is the mind of Christ.

Notes

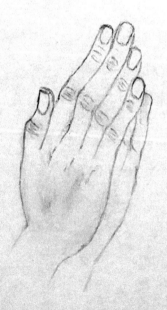

As King

1 Peter 2:9 (NIV)
"But you are a chosen people, a royal priesthood, a holy nation, a people belonging to God, that you may declare the praises of Him who called you..."

Today as I was reading a journal entry in my own journal, I came across something I had written fifteen years ago. The sentence I had written was about prayer and a word caught my eye. In an untidy penmanship I had accidently written the word "asking" as two words— "as king." And today as I stared at my separated word, I saw an ensemble of experiences.

In the religion of shaming, I was taught the lessons that we are nothing, that we should ask for nothing, that we are *worth* nothing, and that God had to make His Son die because of our wickedness. These are the statements I grew up with.

When I lived with Shame I did a lot of crying in prayer. There is no shame in crying, but in Shame we do a lot of crying. In the lies of Shame, I felt desperate. Meager. Insufficient. Small. You see, we behave in the ways we see ourselves. (As a man thinketh, so is he. Proverbs 23:7)

In the last ten years or so, God has been redeeming me, piece by broken piece. My mind took me through some experiences I've had with the Lord in the last few years—experiences in which the exchanges happened. Experiences that moved me farther from shame and closer to belonging. I remembered scripture passages like 1 Peter 2:6, "See, I lay a stone in Zion, a chosen and precious stone, and the one who trusts in Him will never be put to shame." (NIV)

"Jesus Christ, who is the faithful witness, and the first be-gotten of the dead, and the prince of the <u>kings of the earth</u>. Unto Him that loved us, and washed us from our sins in His own blood, and HATH MADE US KINGS AND PRIESTS unto God, and His Father, to Him be glory and dominion forever and ever. Amen." (Revelation 1:5-6 KJV, *emphasis mine*) That's what our Faithful and True One says of us.

"For the creation eagerly waits for the revelation of the sons of God." (Romans 8:19 NET) How can we benefit the world in our smallness? Who is at the root of the philosophy that says we need to see ourselves as insignificant, not as kings and priests? I'm not talking about humility. I'm talking about the crippling sickness of Shame and incompetence. Should we leave the creation waiting while we wallow in a false humility that is really fear in disguise?

"What shall we say to these things? If God be for us, who can be against us? He that spared not His own Son, but delivered Him up for us all, how shall He not with Him also freely give us all things?" (Romans 8:31-32 KJV)

My prayer life has already been transformed a lot in the last few years, but today I thought, "How would I ask if I were a king? How would a king ask the Lord for what he needed or wanted?"

For sure a king wouldn't cry and plead and meagerly ask for things. A king would ask in confidence, believing. I pondered that.

Prayer: In your prayer time today, perhaps you would like to take the time to ask…"How would my prayers change if I came to God and asked . . . as . . . king?"

Notes

One Talent

Matthew 25:25 (NIV)
"So I was afraid and went out and hid your talent in the ground. See, here is what belongs to you."

Jesus described the kingdom of heaven in chapter 25 with a number of stories. The part about the servant with one talent scares me. The timidity and fear in my own life makes me sit up and take notice of this servant with one talent. Wait—what? Timidity isn't humility? Fear is unrighteous?

Think with me. What is fear? It is a feeling of dread, alarm, panic, and anxiety. Why is that unrighteous? Because of what it causes: confusion. It breeds complacency. It makes us cynical. It keeps us from doing. It makes excuses.

Fear costs us our potential.

Jesus was very clear about the consequences this "worthless" servant got in the Kingdom.

When the voice is the voice of my Savior, I'm not sliced by condemnation. I know this voice well. He has led me through one victory at a time and now He shows me this one. The One who came to lead me out of the POW camp said the servant who cowered in fear was wicked. And lazy.

My programming taught me to buckle under threatening voices. I can easily identify with the one-talent servant when he said, "So I was afraid and went out and hid your talent in the ground. See, here is what belongs to you."

Ok, first of all, no. It belongs to me in terms of responsibility! I'm responsible for what I do with it. The one-talent-servant had a skewed perception of the Master. When we're not in close relationship with someone, we understand neither their intentions nor their expectations.

Sweet Cocoa Bean, if you struggle with the same fear as I did and this servant in Matthew 25 did, let me show you a secret. 1 John 4:18 says there is no fear in love. May I be so bold as to say that you cannot talk yourself out of fear. The way to overcome fear is to saturate your soul with the love of God. Every day. As many times a day as you need to, you nourish that precious soul with the lavish love of the Father.

There is no fear in love and *in* (inside of, surrounded by, in the middle of) love there is no fear. If fear, to you, looks larger than love, you may be on the outside of love looking in. But from the inside of love, facing out, you can wield your solitary talent with great mettle and flair.

Don't be caught hiding when He returns. Step into His love. Take every opportunity to experience it. Think about what you would do if you knew you would not fail. His love is the beefiest Beef Broth of all!

Prayer: Lord, I confess that sometimes I am the fearful servant when you have called me to be the valiant son/daughter of the Most High God. Today as I sit before you at the table, cup outstretched, fill my cup with Your love as I wait. Let me tangibly, physically, feel Your love wash over me and fill me. I need nothing else. I want Your love.

Notes

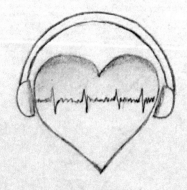

Love With
Your Heart

Deuteronomy 6:5 (ISV)
"You are to love the Lord your God with all your heart, all your soul, and all your strength."

This is a recurring theme in scripture. When Jesus was asked which commandment was the greatest, He quoted this passage.

Today as I read these words, I notice that He says to love the Lord your God with all _YOUR_ heart. This is an important distinction. We are not to love the Lord vicariously through another person. There is something authentic and raw about loving the Lord with _your_ heart. In Matthew 22:34-40 we find the expert of the law who tested Jesus with the question, "Which is the greatest commandment in the law?"

Jesus tested him right back and asked, essentially, "Can you love me with _your_ heart?"

Loving the Lord with our heart requires that we bring it. We can't leave our heart behind. We can't close it. We can't harden it. In all the rawness of who we are and what we've done, and what we've left undone. All the pain. All the questions. All the things that are true. All the victories. All the accomplishments.

The part of you that is original and real. With this we love. With all this we love the Lord.

We're tempted to love the Lord through what we learn or through whom we have learned it. We're often busy searching for the "right" thing to do and the "right" thing to believe. These are important. We *need* to behave in a worthy manner and believe in the right things. But when asked what the greatest was, Jesus said we must make it personal.

In the tests of life, we don't hold up under a loving-the-Lord-through-what-others-have-told-us kind of relationship. With all YOUR heart. With all your soul and with all your strength. You need it to survive the storms.

Prayer: Lord, forgive me for worrying about what others are doing. Help me today to live in my own heart and love you from there. Help me to be present in the moment and deepen my relationship with you. Here is my heart. Warm it and hold it. Let me never stray from loving you in real time.

Notes

Not by Observation

Luke 17:20 (KJV)
"And when He was demanded of the Pharisees, when the Kingdom of God should come, He answered them and said, 'The Kingdom of God cometh not with observation.'"

In this verse, the Greek word paratereo is translated into our English word observation. Paratereo means to stand beside and watch, to stand alongside, to watch oneself or to scrupulously observe.

Sometimes when we're the victim of injustice, especially when the victimizing has gone on for a long time, we feel like we're just a bystander. We watch as someone destroys our life. If we were victimized when we were very young we *didn't* have power over the one who was hurting us. Our brains were trained to be helpless.

Once we were children, but now we're grown-ups. What do we do? We're tired of the abuse but what can we do to get out of it or make it stop? Even as devout Christians we can get stuck in observation mode. We pray and ask God to bring answers. Sometimes we even become demanding with God like the

Pharisees in Luke 17. "When will the Kingdom come?! When will You come to make this stop?!"

Jesus is very moved by the sorrows of His people, no doubt about it, but we need to get involved in our own life. We can't paratereo our lives from a bystander's perspective and expect God to condone our dysfunctional behavior. It is dysfunctional as an adult to abdicate responsibility for our own lives. In Luke 17:21b Jesus hands us a key to unlock one of the gates of our many-gated prison; "the Kingdom of God is within you."

I challenge you to do some research and study what this Kingdom-of-God-within-us is all about. I'd like to share two verses with you. To most of us, these are familiar verses - Matthew 6:33 and Mark 4:11.

"Seek first the Kingdom of God, and His righteousness; and all these things shall be added unto you." (Matt. 6:33 KJV) He's not making petty poetry when He says all these things.

Seek the Kingdom of God. Understand what He's saying here. You have the Kingdom. You don't have to stand outside, alongside of, as though it belonged to someone else. It's yours.

"Unto you is given to know the mystery of the Kingdom of God." (Mark 4:11 KJV) Getting this firmly established in your deepest heart will be one of the first things you need to do as you begin to get a grip on your life. I've watched people, from their own human strength, try to step up and confront their oppressor. But without the Kingdom of God within, we can err on the other side and be hateful, demanding, and repulsive.

In these two little verses Jesus hands us two keys. One: we need to get up and take responsibility for our own well-being, and two: The Kingdom of God is within you.

There are still many doors to unlock, but these two keys will unlock and open places that have up to this point appeared to be solid, doorless walls.

If you have perhaps never taken the step of inviting the Kingdom of God into you, I invite you do so today. With the Kingdom of God within and the Holy Spirit surrounding us, giving us inspiration, together we can move forward. Many discoveries await us. Jesus came to set the captives free.

Prayer: Take a moment—or an hour—to pour out to God your particular situation. Hold nothing back. Tell it all. Tell Him just what you think of the cards you were dealt. And when you have poured it all, wait. Wait for that calm surrender from within you. Surrender. But this time we're not surrendering to the abuse. We surrender to the King of the Kingdom we seek. Ask Him to open your eyes to the mystery He wants to show you—one step at a time. Take the key. Store it safely in your heart.

Notes

Call Unto Me

Jeremiah 33:3 (KJV)
"Call unto me, and I will answer thee, and shew thee great and mighty things, which thou knowest not."

"...which thou knowest not." Small phrases catch my eye.

Curiosity.

A thirst for knowledge.

Hunger.

Call unto Me. I will answer thee.

There have been times when I have hesitated to pray because I didn't know the answer. Isn't that pathetic? Sometimes we forget that we don't know everything.

God says that He WANTS to show us great things. Mighty things. Things we don't yet know about. Think of the possibilities! There are so many solutions to problems. So many angles we can't see from our position. God says, "Hey! Call Me! I'll show you things you haven't seen before. I'll talk to you about answers that haven't crossed your mind."

Struggling to see a way through? Or out? God will literally expand your mind if you ask Him to. He's not even upset that you don't know what to do in your circumstance today. This verse shows us that we are not the one trying to convince God to listen to our plea. God is the one who says to call Him.

Trust that. Come to Him believing He wants to show you great and mighty things. Because He does.

Prayer: Oh Sovereign Lord, give me an instructed tongue, to know the Word that sustains the weary. Wake me morning by morning, waken my ear to listen like one being taught. Oh Sovereign Lord, open my ears that I be not rebellious and that I draw not back from You. (Isaiah 50:4-5)

Notes

An Antidote to Temper Tantrums

Isaiah 55:9 (KJV)

"For as the heavens are higher than the earth, so are my ways higher than your ways, and my thoughts higher than your thoughts."

In desperate times I can get pretty demanding. My prayers sound a bit like temper tantrums, and my spirit is so agitated that my prayers are spewed out in anger. When I think I know exactly how God should answer my prayer, I tend to commence *telling* Him what to do. But God may or may not—mostly not—choose to accommodate such prayers. He may choose to lead us on a wild inquisition across bridges, over rocks, past obstacles, around tree roots and shush us into a reverent hush before He reveals Himself to us. God knows we humans need the hide-and-seek game. He gives us what we need and often not what we want.

If we would get our demanding prayers answered and if we called all the shots, it would put *us* in charge. And if we're in charge, we are also responsible. With responsibility comes blame. We don't want the blame, but we demand answers.

"As high as the heavens are above the earth…" God knows the end from the beginning and we do not. In our limited insight we can make a mess of our lives when we get pushy and demanding. If I think I know so much and want to take charge, and it ends poorly, the humiliating blame is mine.

The real issue, when I get myself worked into a frenzy, is that I need to seek a better way. I need to realize my humble position. God's position and my position are not the same at all! I need to get in a humble posture in my heart and ask God, "God, what is it You want to teach me? My way is not working. Teach me Your way."

God's way is always better and always gives me a better outcome than anything I could think up on my own. He is good and I can trust His plan. I want to settle down and find the way forward to that which He directs me.

Prayer: Lord, as the heavens are higher than the earth, so are Your ways higher than my ways, and Your thoughts higher than my thoughts. Lead me into Your ways. I trust that Your plan is wiser and better and will lead me to a much better place than where I can lead myself.

Notes

The Beauty
of the Lord

John 17:24 (NIV)
"Father I want those You have given Me to be with Me where I am, and to see My glory, the glory You have given Me because You loved Me before the creation of the world."

Did you know that Jesus prayed for you? He prayed generally for all people, but specifically He prayed for you.

To look at the Lord changes us.

"One thing have I desired of the Lord, ...that I may dwell in the house of the Lord all the days of my life *to behold the beauty of the Lord...*" (Psalm 27:4 emphasis added)

To look at the Lord changes us. It changes how we see everything around us. Notice what happens in the rest of Psalm 27. For example, "The Lord is the strength of my life, of whom shall I be afraid." (verse 1) "Now shall my head be lifted up above my enemies round about me..." (verse 6) "Though a host shall encamp against me, my heart shall not fear..." (verse 3)

All this from gazing upon the beauty of the Lord. All this from observing His love for us. When someone looks at us with love on their face, love in their eyes, they appear beautiful to us.

"To behold the beauty of the Lord…" When we look at the Lord, look at His countenance as He looks at us, with love on His face, He is beautiful. I would also say that to behold the beauty of the Lord, to behold His love for me, doesn't mean a quick glance. To behold is to gaze. To contemplate. To give His love time to reach me. To step forward—into it.

What did Jesus pray for? He prayed for those He was given (that's us) to be where He is. Where is He? He is everywhere of course but in every situation, where is He? That's our answer. It's the key. In every situation, to look for Jesus, to look for where He's at work, but most of all to look AT Him. To gain our strength, our safety, our fearlessness, our joy, and more from observing how He loves us.

Then, we will be where He is and we will see His glory, just as He asked the Father that day He sat on a hillside looking up into Heaven, praying—for you.

Prayer: Lord, if my view of You is obstructed, please pull back the curtain, so to speak. One thing I have desired—to see and behold the beauty of Your face, Lord. Pour a fresh cup of strength-giving broth, and I will drink it with thanksgiving.

Notes

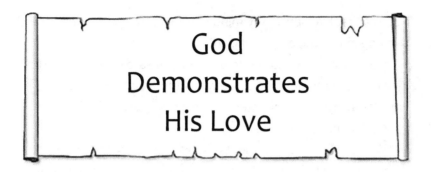

God Demonstrates His Love

Romans 5:8 (NET)
"But God demonstrates His own love for us, in that while we were still sinners, Christ died for us."

Do you ever feel like there is a monster inside? So many feelings? So much pent-up emotion? So much anger that you don't know whether you can keep your self-control? I do. Insecurity is like an internal monster and it feeds on the soul of its host. Aggression and shame, while seemingly opposite, can both feel crippling and overwhelming.

I was in a lively Bible study with my friends one evening when we came across this verse.

God demonstrates His love.

In the group discussion we were happily discussing that to demonstrate is to be active. It's a verb. Action. He doesn't just say He loves us, He acts upon it. As I listened to the ladies, I was staring at the word. I thought, *it's funny that this word almost has the word monster in it*. De-monster. Not exactly in semantic rules, but in a creative sense, my mind was dividing up the word and thinking about the power of God's love.

God's active love comes to us, "while we are yet sinners." His love defuses the anger, disassembles the tough emotions, and whittles away at the monster of insecurity in us.

God demonstrates His love.

While we are yet hostile. While we don't yet know how to overcome. While we still don't know how to clean ourselves up. While we are yet sinners, Christ comes for us. It's His *love* that calms us. His love cleans us. His love melts the anger. His love is that awesome.

In the same way that demonstrate is a verb, so is our receiving of His love. Receiving is a verb. Action. Intentional behavior. Take a moment and observe His love. Watch as it comes near. Give attention to the sense His love brings. Receive it in the center of you.

Prayer: Lord, today I want to breathe You in, and breathe out the tension. Soak me in Your love as I take this moment to give you space. Thank You for Your word. Thank You for Your love. Thank You that this verse is true and that You are true.

Notes

God Is a
Good God

Mark 10:18 (KJV)
"And Jesus said unto him, 'why callest thou me good? There is none good but one, that is God.'"

Jesus was baptized in the Jordan. That's where it all began. The heavy lifting anyway. The hardcore work of His ministry. Where He began what He came to do. In Mark 10, He's back in that area. The Bible says He came to Judea, beyond the Jordan, beyond the point where it all began. I wonder how He got to the other side. I wonder if He rode a ferry across the Jordan. Perhaps there was a boy with a boat charging a lepton per ride for anyone wanting to get to the other side. Being in that place again, I wonder if Jesus was reminded of His 40 days in the desert. Maybe He felt a moment of physical weakness as He remembered that intensely challenging time. Maybe as he ministered to the sick, argued with the Pharisees, and blessed the little children, He fully recognized the unbelievably heavy task at hand—redeeming mankind.

Perhaps it was in thoughts like these, deep in His soul, through which he heard a young man ask the question, "Good Master, what shall I do that I may inherit eternal life?"

Imagine, with the weight of the world on His shoulders, the only shoulders ABLE to purchase eternal life, He looks at the young man and thinks, "Hmmm! What must *you* do? You, my dear Watson, are... why... I'm... *here.*" But like a good Hebrew, He answers a question with a question. "Why do you call Me good?"

In this one question rests the answer to so many of our rough days. Jesus goes on to answer the young man's question with simple reminders of the basic commandments, knowing the young man was already committed to these. It was in the harder part that he faltered. Remember that Jesus had not yet died and risen. They were still operating in the Old Covenant. All that aside, Jesus knew what the man was asking: "Do I have what it takes to make it?" The young man was legitimately seeking peace.

In the question that Jesus asked him, He was giving the young man the clue. I like to imagine this young man was among the 3,000 people who, on the Day of Pentecost in Acts 2, put their faith in the Risen Savior.

Why do you call Me good?

One could only "sell out" to a God who is good. He IS good. We can. But when the days get dark, when the load is heavy, when He asks us to do the hard things, the long list of hard things, the thing that looks impossible, the way forward is to remember the goodness of the One who is asking us to do it.

Why do you call Me good? The answer to that is more than a list of good characteristics we can ascribe to Him. It is also the *experiences* our soul remembers. In the hard times we're naturally drawn to look at the items that are making the difficulties. Before Jesus ever asked the young man to sell out, He asked him to remember why we can know that God is a good God.

In your time of prayer, what is it that you need to reflect on to remind your soul of the goodness of God?

Notes

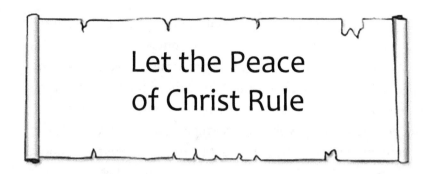

Let the Peace
of Christ Rule

Colossians 3:15 (NIV)
"Let the peace of Christ rule in your hearts, since as members of one body you were called to peace. And be thankful."

In 2013 my life was one continuous trial. In 2013 we were right in the middle of the seven-year-long fight to leave the dysfunction behind. Emotionally my life was in upheaval from many directions. I was resolute in my devotion to God, seeking Him, finding Him, depending on Him, *and* my life was like a small boat, caught in a bad storm on a big sea.

It was in this time that God gave me Col. 3:15; "Let the peace of Christ rule in your heart." Rule.

It says *rule* your heart. It has the meaning of more than just to dwell in or *have* peace, as in the absence of worry. In the Greek the definition holds the picture of an umpire, the deciding one, the director, to rule, govern. In other words, let the peace of Christ umpire your heart. Let the peace of Christ set the rules. This doesn't sound like a life of ease, free of worries. It sounds like we're paying attention, being active, and saying no to evil.

Sometimes there are overwhelming things, many of them,

all coming at us at once! Some of the things are in our control to manage and some of the things are outside of our control. In 2013 there were many things giving me cause to worry that were outside of my personal control but directly affecting me. It felt like the vexations and demands on me were a giant backpack, loaded to bursting with weights hanging on every strap and loop! Through this verse the Lord taught me to let the peace of Christ be the deciding ruler of which worry or responsibility is mine to keep and which one is to be laid aside.

Not every problem that attaches itself to my backpack is mine to carry. The Bible advises us to let peace be the active director of what stays and what gets thrown off. When I determine to live at peace, I will let peace umpire my life. Inside of that peace, I can be productive. I can be busy. I can be clear-headed. I can solve problems. I can definitely be the change I long to see in the world. If I have an overwhelming to-do list and I establish peace as my umpire, I'll be able to command my day in productive activity. If I have to confront someone and peace governs my heart, then what I say will be from peace to create harmony, not more conflict.

Let the peace of Christ rule.

Don't get me wrong! The days that followed were not worry-free! I still had a long way to go before I exited that tumultuous season. I was, however, able to train my mind to set peace as a security guard at the door. As much as I was able, I let peace be in charge so that my internal world was at peace, even though what was going on in the world around me was still far from settled.

Prayer: Lord, I understand peace comes from You. It comes from spending time with You, and it comes from having a clean heart. Clean me today, again; clean my heart every day. I join my soul with this verse and I will determine to let peace rule my life.

Notes

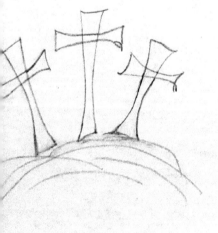

Savior in Our Midst

John 19:18 (ISV)
"There they crucified Him, along with two others, one on each side of Him with Jesus in the middle."

A friend of mine called me recently to ask for some advice. She and her husband were in the middle of a strong disagreement and it had already lasted for days. *He said that I . . . and I said that he . . . But he always . . . And I feel....*

I listened to the all too familiar story of what they were experiencing. It happens to all of us and sometimes those battles can escalate to severe in a short time. Two people who are otherwise mature, productive individuals can get passionately disagreeable and quite a bit blind as to how to resolve the disagreement.

When Jesus was crucified on the cross there were with Him two other people on two other crosses. Two people who had broken the law. Two humans who were put on crosses because of their own failures. Two people who couldn't have been perfect if they had tried with all their mind, soul, and strength. We are those two people.

Jesus, the only perfect and perfectly sinless One, was hanging between them. He was paying the actual price of mercy. Only He could! If the two on either side would have crucified each other, the sin of neither one of them would have been paid for. No one would feel sufficiently relieved of the debt or pain or brokenness they each inflicted on their fellows during a whole lifetime.

Luke 23 records the two cohorts having an argument. Imagine the scene. Two criminals, hanging for their own crimes. The Savior of the world—of *them* in particular—hanging in the middle, not for His own sins, but *theirs*, and the two guys are yelling at each other over the crucified Redeemer.

Whatever grievance we have with each other, trying to extract payment from our counterpart will never truly satisfy the voucher, the running expenditure, incurred against us. And when we point and accuse, we have to point and screech at our fellow-man over the sinless body of Jesus, the Redeemer of both of us. Neither one of us is the sinless Savior. And when we fix our sights on the other human, there is Jesus. In the middle. Dying for the one we're angry at. As well as for me - the other sinner.

Better we fix our gaze on the Savior of us all. Better that we absorb the mercy He extends to *us*, the also guilty one. And better that we ponder on the priceless, perfect gift of His exoneration of *us*, and that the blood He shed for me is the same blood He shed for my spouse. Or anyone else who has offended me. The only perfect One who *could* accuse is the One on the middle cross but even He didn't accuse. He said, "Father forgive them for they know not what they do." The only One perfect and sinless enough to point the finger at sinners, didn't.

Prayer: Oh God, have mercy on me! Me. I am the one in need of mercy. Have mercy on me. Deal with Your other sons and daughters according to Your loving kindness and take this burden of judgment off of my shoulders. I'm in no position to pass judgment on anyone. Only You can.

Notes

Covenant and Contract

Hebrews 8:10 (KJV)

"For this is the covenant that I will make with the house of Israel after those days, saith the Lord; I will put my laws into their mind, and write them in their hearts: and I will be to them a God, and they shall be to me a people."

Covenant and contract. Only a few letters different and only a few words different in definition, but a universe of difference in implementation.

Covenant: (noun) an agreement, usually formal, between two or more persons to do or not do something specified.

Contract: (noun) 1. an agreement between two or more parties for doing or not doing something specified. 2. an agreement enforceable by law.

A covenant is alive with promise and agreement. Two or more people are active in participation. A contract is often used in business, is also between two or more people but is on a formal basis. The two people are not necessarily entering into a relationship as much as they are simply agreeing to a set of transactions with the business deal.

Why do two young siblings get into a fight on the living room floor over who gets the toy? Contract. Two little siblings in covenant will make sure each other have everything they need and are protected. (Not that they are old enough to know these words!)

Why do we get into fights in our marriage? Contract. "You're not holding up your end of the bargain." And especially, "You're not doing what I expected of you." Granted, a lot of times a partner is NOT holding up their end of the agreement, but when confronted in a "contract" way of thinking they aren't usually open to the confrontation. Contract-style arguments lead to both partners adding mud to the discussion until they end up with a mountain of differences piled up between them. Contract in marriage holds the flavor of "enforceable-by-law." Enforceable-by-law holds the effect of "I'm not giving you this until you give me that." How far do two people get in such a conversation? Both end up feeling like they got swindled.

I looked up the word covenant in the Bible. The King James Version mentions covenant in 272 verses. I typed in the word contract and got: "0 verses found." God doesn't deal with us in contracts. He lovingly invites us into covenant with Him.

Jesus often scolded the religious leaders for their contractual modus operandi. And we also get into trouble when we move from covenant to contract. When I'm a contractual Christian, I am measuring and counting. Judging and keeping records of wrong. Where is my joy? Gone. Like a vapor in the wind. The contract presents itself to us as a way to happiness when it doesn't have happiness to offer! Covenant has the warmth of a living heartbeat. Covenant carries promise—two people watching out for each other to make sure the other has what he or she needs. In relationships, covenant and contract are as different as life and death. The surest way to kill a friendship is to apply the contract mentality.

James 3:14-17 paints a great picture of the difference. "...if ye have bitter envying and strife in your hearts, glory not, and lie not against the truth. This wisdom descendeth not from above, but is earthly, sensual, devilish. For where envying and strife is there is confusion and every evil work. But the wisdom that is from above is first pure, then peaceable, gentle, and easy to be entreated, full of mercy and good fruits, without partiality, and without hypocrisy." (KJV)

So whether we are small children, friends, married people, or Christians in relationship with God, consider the difference in covenant and contract and live at peace, Buttercup.

Prayer: Lord, I want to mindfully be in covenant with You. Through that, help me encourage a covenant relationship with my loved ones. Through Your wisdom from above, help me to be flexible *and* virtuous.

Notes

_____

_____

_____

_____

_____

_____

_____

_____

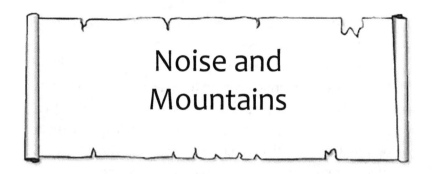

Noise and
Mountains

Isaiah 54:10 (NIV)
"Though the mountains be shaken and the hills be removed, yet my unfailing love for you will not be shaken nor my covenant of peace be removed, says the Lord, who has compassion on you."

Mountains departing.

Some translations use shaken, and some use depart to describe what's happening to the mountain. I understand mountains and hills to be those places of difficulty and obstacles and annoyances and everything not good. In Mark 11:23 Jesus reminds us to speak to the mountain and tell it to be cast into the sea.

I don't suppose mountains would silently vanish away. I imagine they won't go without some noise.

A gas company put an oil well in the field right next to our house. The noise, commotion, and activity it took to install an oil well was quite an ordeal. Large earth movers came in and removed a sizable section of the hillside. Tank trucks brought supplies, and there was a crew of about 15 men on the site for days. Weeks. They built what looked like a little city on the site where eventually the well would be. Point is that not a thing about all that earth-moving was quiet.

Some of the "mountains" in our lives might go quietly. Some might only need a stern command to go and they go. But if the metaphor is kept in a real comparison and if we think about the real events in our lives, it's more consistent with our trials to recognize that some "mountains" just don't go without a fight.

If you are currently "excavating" some unwanted, abusive, or otherwise debilitating mountain out of your life, don't be surprised at the mess it makes during removal. You might choose to keep your mountain and only remove the briars and sharp rocks. This too can be a painful process. Don't lose heart, my friend. "...yet my unfailing love for you will not be shaken nor my covenant of peace be removed, says the Lord, who has compassion on you."

God is telling us that His covenant with us is secure in our insecure environment. The mountains are moving. There's noise. There's resistance. There's all the tactics the mountains use to stay in power over you, but take heart. Keep speaking. Keep moving. The covenant you have with God is a covenant of peace and He will stay with you while you establish this peace in your real life.

Prayer: (Psalm 25 is a great prayer. The following are some cups of broth from this Psalm.)

Oh my God, I trust in You. Let me not be ashamed. Let not my enemies triumph over me. Show me Your ways, oh Lord. Teach me Your paths. Lead me in Your truth. I wait for You all day long. Remember Thy mercies and Thy lovingkindness that You have always had. Mercy and truth belong to those who keep your covenant and testimony. He shall dwell at ease and inherit the earth. Keep my soul, and deliver me. Let me not be ashamed for I put my trust in You.

Notes

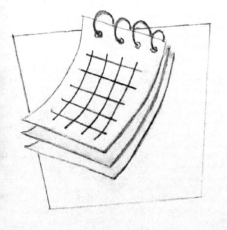

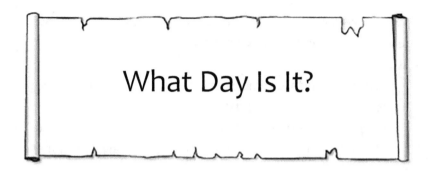

What Day Is It?

Psalm 62:1-2 (KJV)
"Truly my soul waiteth upon God: from Him cometh my salvation. He only is my rock and my salvation; He is my defense; I shall not be greatly moved."

Ever feel greatly moved and deeply disturbed by the dysfunction and destructive behaviors of others? Ever feel like their ugly accusations need to be proven untrue?

"My soul waiteth upon God." In this verse, the Hebrew word to wait has the meaning of silence and stillness as we wait. How is it that we can be silent and still and wait in times when the enemy uses all the people around us to throw insults, accusations, and blame at us?

"My salvation comes from Him." There is a time to do spiritual battle and there is a time to sit in silence while we wait. A close walk with Him is vital to our survival and victory. He will tell us what day it is.

This Psalm was written by King David. I'm amazed by King David for many reasons. The main one is that regardless of how many battles he encountered, he would never attack the enemy army without first consulting God. He was a man of war. If anyone knew how to win, it would be an expert like David. But he never relied on his own wit. He would ask God if, how, and when to attack.

In Psalm 62 he takes time to sit in silence. This sitting in silence is not time wasted. It is mandatory.

What day is it in your life? Have you fought well and need to rest? How do we rest? We rest knowing that our salvation comes *from Him*.

"He only is my Rock." Our rock is not our own wit. Our rock is not our education. Our rock is not another person. He alone is truly our solid rock.

"He is my defense." If we're busy running back and forth arguing and defending ourselves, we're not only worn out, we're also not making space for God to show Himself strong on our behalf. The Word says, "He is my defense." Trusting in God, standing firm on His rock-solid reputation, with unshaken faith that our salvation comes from Him, we will not be greatly moved. No matter with what activity the enemy wears himself out, strutting and puffing all around us, if God has given us the motion to stop and be still, we can be sure of what day it is: a day to be silent and wait for God.

Prayer: Lord, tell me what day it is. I choose to make space to hear from You. Teach me when to stand, when to fight, and when to be silent. I commit my ways to You. You are my Rock, my salvation, and my God. I wait for Your signal. For Your command. Be silent, my soul; wait on the Lord.

Notes

Truth and Grace

John 1:14 (ISV)
"The Word became flesh and lived among us…full of grace and truth."

I once heard of a man who was visiting his cousin in another state. As they sat at dinner in the cousin's home, there was suddenly a thunderous noise outside. The man jumped to his feet, convinced that a tornado was about to rip the house away from around him. The cousin calmly asked what the matter was.

The man stared at his cousin in disbelief. "Don't you hear that tornado?!"

"What tornado?" asked the cousin, as the train engineer pulled the chain on his whistle sounding a long and forlorn call as his train rumbled on past the humble, country home.

The man sank back into his chair, weak from the adrenaline rush leaving his body. "A train!" was all he could say.

His cousin, amused at the reaction he just witnessed, explained, "We don't even hear it anymore. At first when we moved into this house we thought we made a mistake. The train was unbearable. The neighbors around here assured us that we would get used to it. We didn't believe them, but I can see now that they were right."

This morning I read John 1:14 and stopped to ponder this phrase—full of grace and truth. How many times have I read over that and missed "the train outside my window"? I thought, wait a minute. What was truth to them at the time? The Old Testament—the Law. We call the new dispensation the dispensation of Grace! So John was reaching back and bringing in the old, and reaching forward, grabbing the new, and tying them together in Jesus. Verse 17; "For the law was given by Moses, but grace AND truth came by Jesus Christ!"

He IS who you thought He was . . . And MORE!

The tension between the law and grace shows up a lot in a difficult relationship. Do I extend grace and accept the bad behavior? Do I lay down the law and make concrete boundaries? In Jesus we have both the law *and* grace. He is not unjust. He is not jello. He is Jesus—the Word made flesh. He walks *with* us. He is both soft *and* strong. But He is never unjust.

As we walk with this unbreakable truth-and-grace-Jesus, He will teach us His way. God is reckless in His love, but never irresponsible. He accepts risks and danger and demands respect. The truth sets me free when I bring it down and live it, speak it, believe it, experience it.

Prayer: Lord, open my eyes to see where You are. Teach me to observe the contents of the cup I drink from. What is true? What is not? Am I drinking the poison of a lie the enemy is feeding me? Am I drinking in the truth? Teach me Your way, Lord. I want the stability of Truth and Grace.

Notes

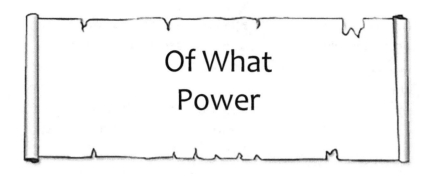

Of What Power

Daniel 10:19 (NET)
"He said to me, 'Don't be afraid, you who are valued. Peace be to you! Be strong! Be very strong!' When he spoke to me, I was strengthened. I said, 'Sir, you may speak now, for you have given me strength.'"

In this scene, Daniel had been in prayer for three weeks about an issue, and on this day he had gone for a walk beside the river. Someone from heaven appeared to him and, as usual, the sheer power and enormity of this being took his strength away and pretty much knocked him out.

Notice how the kingdom of heaven operates. Jesus tells us in John 18:36 that His kingdom is not of this world. It isn't. I've been keeping my eyes open for clues about the kingdom of heaven. If we are to pray, "Let Thy kingdom come," we might do better at praying it if we knew what the kingdom of heaven was. I found a clue here in Daniel. Notice that the powers from heaven—whether it's Jesus, or an angel, or a man in white linen—the powers from heaven don't knock us down with their strength just to knock us down, or just to exercise their power over us for their own pleasure.

In all the accounts in the Bible where heaven's power shows up on the scene, scary as it was to see it, the people either passed out or fell facedown. But the diplomat from heaven *always* helped them back up. Usually they say, "Fear not," even though we always fear. It's as if they are saying, "I know I'm scary, but don't be afraid; I'm on your side." They announce who they are and why they are there and, in essence, say, "Together we'll go after _____" (fill in the blank). Sometimes it's a call to duty, like Moses. Sometimes it's a call to war, like Gideon. Sometimes it's a call to carry something, like Mary. But always the power is helpful and stays with us, so that *together* we get the job done.

In contrast, notice that the narcissistic power will knock you down for simply the dark pleasure of doing so. And notice the other things in life, in your life. In your conversations, are you operating in the kingdom of heaven where you use your strength to "come-along-side-of" or are you, at times, arguing simply to get the upper hand or for the sake of proving the other one wrong? To take their power away because it makes you feel better.

Also, in the conflicts you are in currently, would it help to sort them out if you weighed them on this scale? Are you being overcome by others simply by their hunger for power? It's not unusual that a Christian gets confused by submission. After all, we are taught to turn the other cheek and to go the second mile for people. But sometimes our existence is filled with such neurotic chaos that we get deeply entangled in the webs others weave for us. We are called to bring the kingdom of heaven to earth. We are not called to operate in the dark power of the kingdom of darkness NOR to submit to it. May each of us be blessed with the gentle, powerful diplomacy of heaven as we navigate our way through the negotiations we make here on Earth.

Prayer: "Our Father, who is in heaven, Hallowed be Your name. Your kingdom come, Your will be done, on earth as it is in Heaven" (Matthew 6:9-10). Oh Lord, teach me today to know the difference and to recognize the power at work around me. Help me to stand up against the darkness and to bring the helpful power of the kingdom of heaven. Come to me, strengthen me as you strengthened Daniel. Feed me from your eternal pot of sustaining broth.

Notes

Stepping In

John 5:4 (KJV)
"For an angel went down at a certain season into the pool and troubled the water: whosoever then first, after the troubling of the water, stepped in was made whole of whatever disease he had."

In Jerusalem was a pool. A special one. Not the American public swimming pool with chlorine and blue dye where everyone is hanging out having a relaxing time in the sun. I don't know if the water in this pool was blue or clear, but I know that the pool was surrounded by porches. Five porches. These porches were covered colonnades to provide shade from the heat of the sun and a shelter from inclement weather. John says a great number of people hung out among the porches at this pool, but not to swim. They were there because they all had physical or mental disabilities.

There is another story about troubled water. (Mathew 14:22-33) The Disciples were on the boat and Jesus walked on the troubled water. In some ways it seems that the storm in Mathew 14 was prepared with a purpose. In the end God was glorified and the faith of the disciples was definitely increased.

Back in Jerusalem it says an angel came at a *certain* time. I don't know if you've had "certain" times, but I have. There was this one certain time that . . . And then this other certain time that . . . You know the times. Those times when your whole world got rattled. The day you got the news that changed your life. For some it's the day their spouse announced they want out of the marriage. For some it was the day their child's life was tragically ended. For some it was the day they had the mental breakdown. You know the "certain" time. The time *your* pool got stirred. The day something outside of your control blew in and shook the place where you've been hanging out.

Do you find it interesting that it says the first person to *step in* was made whole? We typically want to run—or fight. But to *step in*? I mean, Peter did, but Peter was crazy and did crazy things all the time. He saw Jesus walking on the water and asked if he could get out of the boat and join Him. I'm sure Peter learned a lot that day.

What does it mean to step in? To lean in. When things are disturbing and our world has gone into a tailspin, what does it mean to *step in*? The first person in is the one who is made whole. Could we also surmise that the sooner we step in the sooner we're made whole?

I, of course, don't mean wallowing. No health ever came of groveling and wallowing. Stepping in is not an increase of your own hysteria. I suggest that stepping in is the opposite of avoiding. Stepping in is running straight *to* God. Stepping in is stepping up. It is leaning in to learn.

What if *your* troubled pool is the best opportunity that life could have handed to you because it reveals to you your distinct issue, where your weakness is. Or it simply provides you with the urgent need to dig deeper. To grow stronger. To develop higher skills. To seek healing. To begin a path toward greater wholeness—of mind, of faith, of health, of relationship. The first one in gets healed.[1]

Prayer: Courage. Today, Lord, if I lack courage to face what I need to face, please fill my cup with a ladle of courage.

Notes

---

[1] This is not a discussion of whether God sends the trials or whether you bring them on yourself, or if the trial is from the devil. This discussion is solely about using everything that is given to you for good and about using the storm's own force to propel you to a better place.

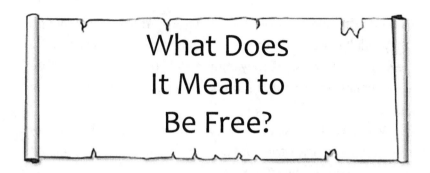

What Does It Mean to Be Free?

John 8:32 (MKJV)
"And you shall know the truth, and the truth shall make you free."

What does it mean to be free?

I grew up hearing John 8:32 used a lot, but often in the sense of "why aren't you free already? The truth shall make you free!" Maybe in a works-centered mind, freedom is something one needs to get done.

Today we will extract some "broth" from John 8:31-40, Galatians 4, and John 1.

John 8:36 "Therefore if the Son shall make you free, you shall be free indeed." (MKJV) I've heard people in my life use this verse as, "I don't have to do what you (or they) ask, because I'm free." Maybe to a rebellious mind freedom is "the prize."

The question remains. What does it mean to be free? Free from what? Free **to** what? In America we have the song "Don't Worry, Be Happy." We have the 60's. We have Generation Y. Is freedom a release from responsibilities?

What are we free from and what are we free to? Even though they didn't understand the new birth, or the New Covenant, the Jews got it. In verse 33 they immediately began arguing whose descendents they were. Freedom, to them, was a slavery/sonship issue.

Verse 34: Jesus said, "Whoever practices sin is the slave of sin." Verse 35: "The slave does not abide in the house forever, but the son abides forever." (MKJV)

"The heir, as long as he is a child, is no different from a slave, though he is the owner of everything, but he is under guardians and managers until the date set by his father. In the same way we also, when we were children, were enslaved to the elementary principles of the world. But when the fullness of time had come, God sent forth His Son . . . to redeem those who were under the law, so that we might receive adoption as sons . . . you are no longer a slave, but a son; and if a son, also an heir of God through Christ." (Gal.4:1-7 ESV)

"To all who did receive Him, who believed in His name, He gave the right to become children of God..." (John 1:12 ESV)

Somehow that takes the fight out of me. If I am my mother's daughter, I don't have to argue my position. No outside agent of any size can negate it.

I am my Father's child. Jesus established that. He adopts us as we are, but as children grow, so we grow into handling the estate we own.

Ever feel defensive and hostile? As sons we are free from the need to defend, fight, and argue. Security.

If the Son sets you free, you will be free indeed. What is freedom? What are you free from? What are we free to? We are sons. We are the daughters. We belong. As sons and daughters, the table is ours. We have a permanent place of belonging and the resources our Father has are ours. We are free from shame. We are free from "other owners" (i.e. the law, other gods, whims). We are free to roam the cabin. Free to explore the Kingdom. Free to discover our calling. Free to sit in our Father's house and spend time with Him. Free to ask Him anything we want. Free to take on His name.

Free to ... belong.

I invite you to sit with this devotion and let your own prayer flow.

Notes

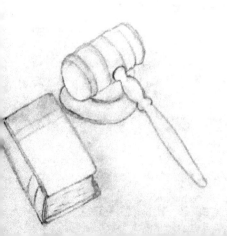

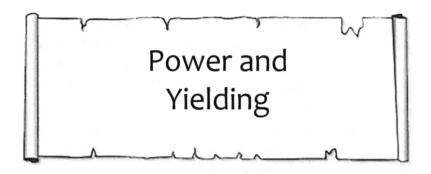

Power and Yielding

Romans 6:16 (KJV)
"Know ye not, that to whom ye yield yourselves servants to obey, his servants ye are to whom ye obey..."

A lot of times when I read the New Testament commands of (or demands for) holiness, I feel so utterly unable to attain such colossal goals.

Ephesians 1:19-20 is part of a prayer that Paul prayed for us. He prayed that we would know the exceeding greatness of His power—the power that raised Christ from the dead. This power is for us.

If all the power that raised Christ from the dead is *available*, why can't I reach the goal of holy living spelled out in the writings of the Apostles? Why am I cross with the kids? Why am I still servant to my hormones? The ups. The downs. The moods. The energy. The lack of energy. I try so hard and yet I fail. I need this power. I need it in my parenting. I need it at my job. I need it in my prayers.

"Know ye not, that to whom ye yield yourselves servants to obey, his servants ye are to whom ye obey..." Is the answer then in the yielding?

Our own righteousness is unacceptable anyway, (See Isaiah 64:6) so, I have a feeling we can't "do well enough" to attain special favors, or to be given the power that raised Christ from the dead. Trying hard has one sort of attitude. Yielding has a whole other attitude about it.

". . . to whom ye yield yourselves servants to obey, his servants ye are . . ." If I try in my flesh to do the commands He sets in His Word, am I not then, still, the servant of my flesh?

Yielding to God . . . How is that done in practical motion? This is a question we can ponder as we go about our days. What does it look like to yield to God? What is He asking you to do? In what *direction* is He asking you to yield?

This morning I was reading in John 6:47-59. "As the living Father has sent Me, and I live through the Father, so he who partakes of Me, even he shall live by Me." (Verse 57 MKJV) This sounds like yielding.

Ideally, the communion elements are unleavened bread and grape juice (or wine). But I have been in places where I have had some very unconventional items on hand and used them! If you have anything resembling bread without yeast, and anything liquid that is grape or made of fruit, I encourage you to grab them as we continue together today. Our "sip of broth" will be taking communion with the Lord.

Prayer: Lord, in surrender to Your Word, I take this, Your body, and this, Your blood, and I eat it and drink it, at Your command. Thank you for Your life in me. I yield to You. Even today as I go about my business, I ask that You show me how to yield, and what that looks like. I want to live in that exceeding power that is for us who believe. To overcome. To endure to the end. And to live to my fullest purpose.

Notes

Have in Mind
the Things
of God

Matthew 16:23 (NIV)
"Jesus turned and said to Peter, 'Get behind me, Satan! You are
a stumbling block to me; you do not have in mind the things of
God, but the things of men.'"

Way back in the day, when Joshua and the Israelites were march-
ing around Jericho (Joshua 6:10), he forbade the people to speak
for seven days. He knew the people were going to complain and
grumble. It was better not to speak at all. Jericho had a wall
around it so thick that people built their entire house right within
the wall. The directive to march around this wall appeared to be
pretty stupid.

Ever felt like your life was in a stupid place? Ever feel like everything is stupid?

Imagine you were Peter, from today's verse. You were walking along the dirt road with the Messiah, the Savior of the known
world, the answer to all life, and He had suddenly stopped and
said that He would be killed soon. That would sound pretty stupid.

If you had been Peter, you would have cashed in all your hopes and dreams on this one man, Jesus. But now He says, "Nope, I'm gonna die. And real soon." (Keep in mind the New Testament wasn't written yet. We have to give our man Peter some credit.)

Peter, with his entrepreneurial mind and quick tongue, grabbed at what came natural to him, and declared, "That will never happen!"

Sometimes God's ways are so vastly different from our ways that His ways sound unreasonable to us. Who marches around a city expecting it to collapse because of a silent walk? When our life doesn't make sense we naturally turn to complaining and grumbling. Shoot! We're so good at it that if no one listens to us, we can play both parts! We can easily complain to ourselves, and in turn, feel sorry for ourselves. Who needs people? We can do this on our own!

But if we want victory...

Let's go back to where Peter went off the rail. The key is in the last part of our verse today. Jesus said, "You do not have in mind the things of God, but the things of man." He gave His disciples a little speech after that and ended by saying that there were some of them that would not taste death before they saw Him coming in His kingdom.

Cocobean, He came so that we can trade in our small-mindedness for Kingdom minds. Minds that can hear and perceive instructions, regardless of how odd they sound. Minds that are on the things of God, and not on the things of men. The disciples were able to receive a new mind and they did! Long before they left this earth.

Joshua's people had to be silent until they could shout in victory. My friend, if you find yourself caught in a negative spiral of complaining and griping, just stop. Quit talking. You'll talk yourself right out of the miracle. If you can't declare the praises of God, go silent until you can.

Prayer: Lord, I don't want to sin and I don't want to rob myself of the miracle that wants to happen. I bring my smallness to you. I ask to trade it in for a Kingdom mind. Set a watch on my mouth. Today may I speak Your words or no words at all.

Notes

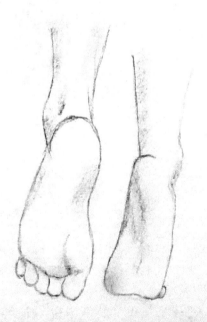

Under Your Feet

Romans 16:20 (ISV)
"The God of peace will soon crush Satan under your feet. May the grace of our Lord Jesus, the Messiah, be with all of you!"

(Sob) My feet? Can't you use someone else's feet? Or a hammer? Shoot. A freight train has no feelings. Can you crush him with a freight train? Why my feet?

Many times we rush to the victory celebration part of this verse, shouting and proclaiming that God will crush Satan soon. Yay! Hallelujah! But today as I look at this verse, I see the alarming truth that the combat zone, the piece of real-estate where this crushing takes place, is under *my feet*. Do you know what this means, Gentle Warrior?

This means the blood and guts of the crush will stain *me*. I'm not in the grandstands as a spectator. I'm *in the ring*! All the jagged, pointy remains of a victory, there, under my feet. It hurts. I look up at the tear-stained face of my Lord. This hurts, Jesus!

He knows it does. He's also there. With me. The second half of the verse says, "May the grace of our Lord Jesus, the Messiah, be with all of you!" Yeah, Imma need that! In the ring, on the battleground, fear costs too much. Fear will cost me everything. To turn and run when it's time to fight will cost me everything I hold dear. I must fight. I must obey every command of the Lord. I must make every move exactly as He says.

"For our struggle is not against human opponents, but against authorities, cosmic powers in the darkness around us, and evil spiritual forces in the heavenly realm. For this reason, take up the whole armor of God so that you may be able to take a stand whenever evil comes. And when you have done everything you could, you will be able to stand firm." (Ephesians 6:12-13 ISV) Don't forget who we're fighting against and who we're fighting *for*. We fight FOR our loved ones and AGAINST the loathsome evil one. But fight we must. The God of Peace will crush Satan under our feet. May the grace of our Lord Jesus, the Messiah, be with all of you!

Prayer: *(Based on Eph 6:14-18)* Lord, I solemnly ask for the belt of truth, the breastplate of righteousness, the boots of the gospel of peace, the shield of faith, the helmet of salvation, and the sword of the Spirit. Make me alert and diligent as I pray and battle for all my fellow saints.

For your reading enjoyment I have added a copy of the United States Uniformed Service's Oath of Office:

I, [name], do solemnly swear (or affirm) that I will support and defend the Constitution of the United States and the Constitution of the State (Commonwealth, District, Territory) of ___ against all enemies, foreign and domestic; that I will bear true faith and allegiance to the same; that I will obey the orders of the President of the United States and the Governor of the State (Commonwealth, District, Territory) of ___, that I make this obligation freely, without any mental reservations or purpose of evasion, and that I will well and faithfully discharge the duties of the Office of [grade] in the (Station and District, Territory of ___) on which I am about to enter, so help me God.

Notes

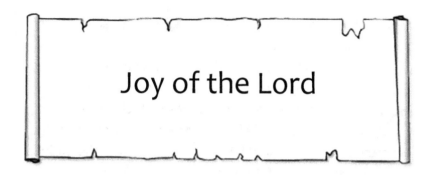

Joy of the Lord

Nehemiah 8:10 (KJV)
". . . for the joy of the Lord is your strength."

Joy has been a struggle for me. I love things that are funny. I love to laugh. I do. But joy . . . retaining joy, feeling joyful, has been a struggle for me. Maybe because I feel things deeply, I also feel pain deeply. I have even had a sense of guilt at times for behaving joyfully when I know that there is so much distress in the world. Do I have a right to be joyful when others are suffering in sorrow right now? These are the thoughts that plague a gentle warrior's soul.

Great things happen in my kitchen. One day a friend of mine was spending the afternoon with me. The sights and aromas we were cooking up that day were indeed enough to bring even the saddest heart some joy. We were discussing the verse, "…the joy of the Lord is your strength."

"Did you know," she said to me, "that 'the joy of the Lord' has a prepositional phrase and that it's the *Lord's* joy that gives us strength?"

The stirring spoon in my hand nearly dropped to the floor.

"Do you know that you're right?!" I finally said as I absorbed the meaning of what she said.

My friend and I are both mothers. We both are well aware of the joy and pride we feel when we watch our children doing well. We both have seen plenty of the opposite. We've experienced the debilitating effects of shaming. As we discussed the difference, the contrast was stark! We imagined, together, the smiling, pleased countenance of Papa God as He gazed at his daughters, together, cooking a meal to share with others later. We could see that, yes, if directed TO us, there would be strength in having the joy of the Lord, the approval of our Father in heaven, and the pride He feels when we do well.

The Lord loves us all, but in a relationship where He tells you, personally, what to do and you do it, you *feel* it. You feel His approval and this is strength to you.

This was a relief to me, for several reasons. I don't have to fabricate joy within myself! It doesn't matter how I feel. It matters that He's proud of me! I have something to do in that. How I choose to behave is my responsibility. I have choices! I can choose to make my Papa proud and in His pride I feel His affection for me and it's the *joy of the Lord* that will give me strength.

"Jesus, for the joy set before Him, endured the cross…" (Hebrews 12:2 KJV) We can do ANYTHING if we keep in mind that ultimately it doesn't matter how we feel. It matters that we do our Father proud!

The joy my friend and I felt at this discovery was enough to make us a little giddy. I dare say the flavor of the food we were preparing improved because our Papa was there in the kitchen with us, smiling and feeling pleased as two of His daughters grew in their knowledge of Him.

Prayer: Thank you, Heavenly Father, for your joy and your strength. *"Therefore, my heart is glad, my whole being rejoices, and my body will dwell securely." Psalm 16:9 (ISV)* Thank you, Lord, that I belong to You and that You care about what I do.

Notes

Not by Sight

2 Corinthians 5:7 (KJV)
"For we walk by faith, not by sight."

Developing a set of spiritual senses is vital to an overcomer.

One morning I chose the front patio to be my study spot. It was a beautiful morning. Summer was just beginning. The birds were singing. The whole outdoors was alive and busy.

I was reading in Hebrews that morning and arrived at chapter 11, verse 3; "By faith we understand that the universe was formed at God's command, so that what is seen was not made out of what was visible." (NIV)

Maybe it was because I had just filled all my senses with the amazing sights, sounds, and smells of my bright summer morning in the country. Maybe it was the way this translation put it. Whatever it was, I stopped on that verse and reread it. "By faith we understand that the universe was formed at God's command, so that what is seen was not made out of what was visible."

I looked at all the things around me. The fluffy white clouds floating across a hazy blue sky. The tall trees. The intricate design of the leaves that covered all my tall trees. I saw the grass - each blade alive with shimmering green beauty. I looked at the pebbly stones covering my driveway, the soft flower petals in the flower pot beside me. My eyes went back to the hazy blue sky and I pondered on the universe that was beyond the blue dome.

I read again, slowly, "By faith we understand that the universe was formed at God's command, so that what is seen was not made out of what was visible." It took my breath away.

"So we do not lose heart. Though our outer self is wasting away, our inner self is being renewed day by day. For this light, momentary affliction is preparing for us an eternal weight of glory beyond all comparison, as we look not to the things that are seen but to the things that are unseen. For the things that are seen are transient, but the things that are unseen are eternal" (2 Corinthians 4:16-18 ESV).

Suddenly a lot began to make sense to me. We are born onto this planet and live in our bodies, but if what is visible to our physical eyes was made from that which is not seen, then . . . we walk by faith and not by sight!

Are you facing an impossible situation? A problem for which you *see* no solution? If the UNIVERSE was made at God's command, but not from what is visible, then, Hello! He can make for me the way through my impossibility ALSO from what is not visible to me!

My prayers just lost their ceiling.

Notes

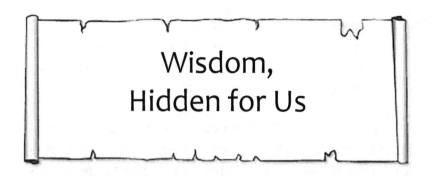

Wisdom, Hidden for Us

I Corinthians 2:7 (KJV)
"But we speak the wisdom of God in a mystery, even the hidden wisdom, which God ordained before the world unto OUR glory." (emphasis added)

"We, of course, have plenty of wisdom to pass on to you once you get your feet on firm spiritual ground, but it's not popular wisdom, the fashionable wisdom of high-priced experts that will be out-of-date in a year or so. God's wisdom is something mysterious that goes deep into the interior of his purposes. You don't find it lying around on the surface. It's not the latest message, but more like the oldest—what God determined as the way to bring out his best in us, long before we ever arrived on the scene. The experts of our day haven't a clue about what this eternal plan is. If they had, they wouldn't have killed the Master of the God-designed life on a cross. That's why we have this Scripture text: No one's seen or heard anything like this, never so much as imagined anything quite like it—what God has arranged for those who love Him." (1 Cor. 2:6-10 The Message Bible)

I want to tell you about something. Have you ever been part of an event, say, maybe a company Christmas party, or a child's birthday party, where gifts are being handed out? In the process of a company Christmas party, one might hear, "This is for you, this is for you, and here, this one is especially for you." At a child's birthday party, all the children might be given special toys to play with, but the birthday child is given the special gifts that the guests had prepared in advance to give to the one who is being celebrated.

I had an event in my home where my mother handed out her treasured heirlooms to all of us children. Pieces that were especially meaningful to me became mine to keep. I have those pieces in my house now.

Today when I read 1 Cor. 2:7 the word "our" became the operative word. There's a glory that belongs to the angels, a glory that is God's glory, and a glory that belongs to Jesus. And here in Corinthians, we see that before He created time as we know it here on earth, God prepared something special *for us*. A glory that is ours.

This one belongs to *us*. The Message Bible accurately says, "the Spirit, not content to flit around on the surface, dives into the depths of God, and brings out what God planned all along." (1Cor. 2:10)

Are we the birthday child who leaves their gift unopened? I dearly hope not. When we're born again, 1 Cor. 2:12 is true of us. "We have received, not the spirit of the world, but the Spirit which is of God, that we might know the things that are freely given to us of God." (KJV)

One more note about 1 Cor. 2:9. I have heard the argument that if it says "eye has not seen," it also means that "eye will not see" until we get to heaven. That's not what it says. Seen, heard, and imagined become past tense verbs in the English language. In Greek they are just verbs. When we didn't have the Spirit of God inside, we didn't see. It is His joy and delight to hand us the Gift He prepared for us way back when we were a thought in His mind!

The hidden wisdom is for us. We haven't even imagined yet what all God has in store for us. It's not his plan to have us stay ignorant. In the dark. He ordained before the world that His children would have His wisdom.

Prayer: Lord, let my eye see and my ear hear what You have for me. I regret all the days I have left my gift from You unopened on the table. I'm so sorry. Let me pull back the wrapping and peer into this priceless, treasure box of wisdom before me.

Notes

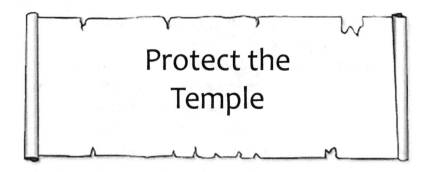

Protect the
Temple

1 Corinthians 3:16 (NIV)

"Don't you know that you yourselves are God's temple and that God's Spirit lives in you?"

Have you ever just felt oppressed and overrun with rubbish? Like you just had junk piled up in your soul? Like your thoughts were heavy and like your mind was invaded by a darkness? I had a morning like that. I woke up early and before I even had time to think my own thoughts, I felt the sludge of this oppression.

I reached for my Bible and it opened to the story in John 2:15 where Jesus made a whip out of cords and drove animals and people out of the temple. My mind saw the scene. I grew up on a small farm. The sights and sounds in a barn are familiar to me. There is dust everywhere. Animals make noise and rarely hold still. They mill about, pushing, and shoving against each other. They eat and leave droppings. John chapter 2 also says there were people in the scene, buying, selling, and negotiating bargains.

I thought, *that's exactly how I feel this morning! I feel like my soul is not my sacred space right now! It's crowded with noise, confusion, voices, bickering, and contention.* I had felt sullen even before I was fully awake.

I thought of the verse that states that *we* are the temple. I said to Jesus, "Yes, I am the temple of God. Drive out of ME these things that are crowding in to make me feel dirty and dropped upon. Clean out my soul and make me, again, a sacred place where You and I can meet and talk clearly, in peace."

I physically *felt* the cleansing! My spirit was thrilled to be relieved of the dirt and clamoring! You see, sometimes we feel bad because we have sinned and defiled our temple. But sometimes we are simply overrun by trespassing spirits and people. Either way, Jesus feels today as He did then. He's very supportive of our desire to have a clean temple.

People are all too willing to take advantage of us and behave toward us as if they own us and like we owe it to them to make our life be all about them. But Jesus doesn't support that. He wants us to have peace inside. To have a sacred and clean temple that can be used as a house of prayer at any moment.

I remember this day very clearly. I did not feel like Jesus was angry *with me* that day. The whip in His hand was not to whip *me*. He was angry against the invaders. He showed up FOR me, not against me.

Prayer: Create in me a clean heart, Oh God. (Psalm 51:10) Lord, I know I cannot clean myself. I come to you for that. Today I ask You to drive out of my temple anything that defiles and clutters up the space that is to be Your space in me.

Notes

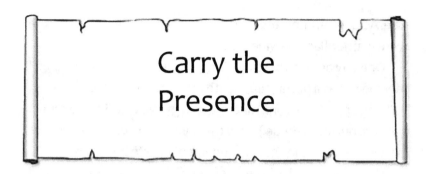

Carry the Presence

Mark 2:22 (ISV)
"And no one pours new wine into old wineskins. If he does, the wine will make the skins burst, and both the wine and the skins will be ruined. Instead, new wine is poured into fresh wineskins."

> When God's people get it right,
> The whole world wins.
> When God's people get it wrong,
> The whole world loses.

I've made wine. It's not hard to do but it requires careful attention. During the fermentation stage and the "new wine" stage, the wine is very fizzy. The covering of your jar has to be porous or the pressure will shoot the lid to the ceiling, spraying juice, bits of grapes, and bubbles all over the cupboards and ceiling. Don't ask me how I know this!

New wine fizzes.

We could go into an extended history lesson here, but for the sake of your time, let's keep it short. The wine is the Holy Spirit (see Acts 2). And before there were fancy glass bottles, there were leather flasks—wineskins.

One day as I was reading Mark 2, I saw the story in motion. I saw the fizz as a puffing up—both in the good way (i.e., edifying, building up, encouraging) and in the negative way (i.e. 1Cor. 8:1-3, a proud, puffed attitude.) I saw the skins—old skins as brittle, set in their ways, prejudiced. The judgments in life being set.

Have you ever had the experience of being pressed on all sides until everything you ever believed in is put to the test? Let it. Have you ever been squeezed until it feels like you have to leave your skin to escape the pressure? Let it. Have you ever had to re-examine the answers you once thought were the right ones? Do it. If the Lord is pressing your old skins off (metaphorically), let Him.

In my motion picture of Mark 2, I saw that if we'd pour New Wine into old wineskins, it would "puff" us "up" in our own self-righteousness, filling the nooks and cubbyholes in our self-important hearts like the air in fermenting wine. Trying to "minister" out of a heart inflated with puffy air, we would make a mess all over the one we're ministering to. It says both the wine and the skins will be ruined.

When God's people get it right,
The whole world wins.
When God's people get it wrong,
The whole world loses.

Let's get it right today, Beautiful. Not everything of the past is good and not every new thing is great. Know the Lord. Let Him make all things new *in* you. New skin can stretch. It can grow to contain the wild and adventurous love of God and true service to people. Changing from our old to the new is sometimes the hardest thing we encounter. The pressing, the squeezing, the crushing, the testing, the peeling away—these are all real. In real time, these things hurt. They confuse us while they're happening. But Dear One, don't give up. Let it happen. Let everything that has ever happened (and is currently happening) work for your good. You will come out the other end a new creation, full of love, carrying the Presence, and able to minister with clarity and goodness.

Prayer: Oh God! Let me see Your face. Let me see what I am to do in this test. Peel the old off of me and make me a true reflection of You. Dip me deep into Your water until I come up clean.

Notes

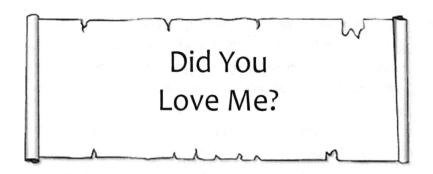

Did You Love Me?

Mark 12:29-30 (MKJV)

"And Jesus answered him, the first of all the commandments is, 'Hear, O Israel, the Lord our God is one Lord; and you shall love the Lord your God with all your heart and with all your soul and with all your mind, and with all your strength.' This is the first commandment."

My precious mother was ill. She couldn't get her breath. My sister's voice on the phone told me it was an emergency situation. My sister was farther away from our mother's house than I was and she asked if I could go help Mom.

Yes. Yes, I could. I flew into action mode and in a short time we were sitting in the waiting room as the doctors and nurses were rushing to get IV's strung and blood drawn for tests. It occurred to me that I had not once stopped to pray. Me? The intercessor who prays a lot had not stopped to pray? This alarmed me more than a bit. How could I have been as neglectful as this?

As I puzzled over this, the Holy Spirit brought a picture to mind. It was a picture I had doodled in church just two weeks prior. The sermon had been on the verse about the most important commandment. I had sketched pictures instead of words.

I had drawn a heart and had invented steam-looking squiggles for the soul. My picture for strength was a muscled arm. My paraphrased verse beneath my art read like this: Love the Lord your God with your feelings, with your thoughts, and with your actions.

The Holy Spirit asked me, "Precisely with which of these did you love Me today concerning your mother?"

Ahhh! Yes. Thank you. Got it. No condemnation. Obedience to the first commandment comes in many forms. Sometimes we get absorbed in believing that one of the four is more important than the other three. God knew that we would. Lest we get mistaken and off course, He spells it out specifically each time this commandment is mentioned. All four are ways in which to love the Lord. One way is not better than another way. All four are part of the holy and first command. All four are equal when it comes to ministry and ministering to others. I had loved my mother with my strength. And in using my strength to get her the help she needed, I had loved the Lord with my actions.

"Hear, O Israel, the Lord our God is one Lord; and you shall love the Lord you God with all your heart and with all your soul and with all your mind, and with all your strength. And the second is like this: you shall love your neighbor as yourself. There is no other commandment greater than these." (Mark 12:29-31 MKJV)

Prayer: Lord, today let these three verses be both the broth and the meat for me. Let me take in the words and meaning until they become part of my DNA.

Notes

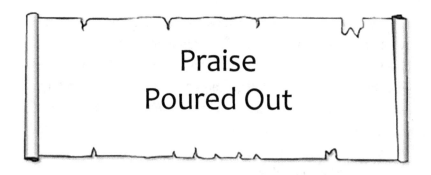

Praise
Poured Out

Luke 7:37 (MKJV)
"And behold, a woman, a sinner in the city, knowing that He reclined in the Pharisee's house, brought an alabaster vial of ointment."

I opened the door of the lovely little coffee shop near my home. The aroma of coffee filled my senses. The aroma of coffee and creamer and sweets filled not only my nose but also my soul. Aroma has meaning. To me coffee means friendship, time with God, special favor, social gatherings, warmth, awareness, and many more things. Coffee reminds me of my mother. It reminds me of the coffee dates I've had with my friends.

Aroma has meaning.

God asked Moses and Aaron to burn incense in the tabernacle. (Ex. 30:7) They were to keep it burning. Every day. Exodus 40:27 calls it sweet incense. Revelation 8 talks about prayers and incense coming up together before God. I wonder what our prayers smell like to God.

The price of the Alabaster perfume has been debated over the centuries. I'm content to know that it was very decidedly pricey. Expensive. It cost her. It wasn't like the woman in Luke 7 would have been able to open her cupboard and choose one of many different jars of ointment. This would have been the only one she had. She would have been saving money for a long time to be able to buy an alabaster vial of ointment. It took planning. Intentional thought and action. Devotion. A long effort toward one goal.

Worship has meaning.

From the story that Jesus told after the incident, we can know that she deeply valued Jesus and treasured the grace and forgiveness that she received. This act of worship wasn't just an act. It was long planned and worked for and it was genuine worship from her heart. A heart full of devotion, gratefulness, and even reckless abandon. "She stood behind Him, weeping at His feet, and she began to wash His feet with her tears and wipe them with the hair of her head. And she ardently kissed His feet and anointed them with the ointment." (Luke 7:28 MKJV)

All this I pondered as I waited my turn to order my jamocha joe. I was so absorbed in the scene at Simon the Pharisee's house that I could almost see their faces and hear the sobbing civilian. I could see her pour out her praise in the form of expensive ointment from the little vial in her hand. It suddenly occurred to me that the weeping worshipper would now also have her costly, pricey, intentional-act-of-worship ointment on her own lips as she bent to kiss the object of her devotion! The very ointment intended for the feet of the Lord she worshipped was now also giving fragrance to her own lips! Aroma has meaning.

"Oh Jehovah, open my lips, and my mouth shall show forth Your praise!" (Psalm 51:15 MKJV)

The sweet girl behind the counter turned to me. "What can I get for you?"

She had the aroma! I wanted to hug her. She must have spent a moment worshipping the Savior on her way to work. It showed. Our worship shows! We carry the fragrance.

Who can tell me the price of worship? What is it worth to you? Is it worth a sacrifice? Is it worth the wholesale cost? I say it is! This and much more! The words of our praise leave the scent of heaven on our lips.

Prayer: "Let my prayer be accepted as sweet-smelling incense in Your presence. Let the lifting up of my hands in prayer be accepted as an evening sacrifice." (Psalm 141:2 GW) Oh Lord! Wash the stench of the world off of me and bathe me in Your Word! Wash me and I will be clean and may my worship fill the room I'm in, everywhere I go. I worship You, Jesus!

Notes

The Door

Luke 12:32 (KJV)
"Fear not, little flock; for it is your Father's good pleasure to give you the kingdom."

We are raising a couple of calves. We made a small barn for their shelter and the doorway is an open doorway. The calves are free to enter and exit their shelter as they please as we didn't put a closing door on the doorway for that very purpose. Our small farm is built into a hillside. Around the other buildings, the landscape is graded to direct the watershed away from the buildings, but the calves somehow manage to reposition the soil around their barn. This makes a constant battle with water issues in the rainy days.

A critter of some kind—I don't know if it's a chipmunk, a rat, or some other small critter—ate a hole through the barn frame. This invading critter put his little drilling construction crew to work, tunneling the hole into the corner of the barn, where the hill meets the barn, letting in the maximum amount of rainwater possible. Keep in mind that the doorway of said barn is twelve FEET away and never closed. This thieving critter could freely come and go through the already provided opening but instead chooses to dig its own door through the wooden framework of the barn.

It's springtime, and where we live, we get rain four days out of seven in most weeks of springtime. I provide sawdust bedding for the calves, and every day this sawdust would get sloppy-soaked with water, because of the hole. A couple weeks ago I bought a can of foaming insulation and sprayed the hole shut. The insulation worked! Until the critter chewed a hole *through it!* Today I nailed a piece of metal siding into that corner! Try chewing through metal, my furry pillager!

As I continued my morning routine of chores, a parable formed in my mind. Our Father in Heaven provides for us. Jesus is the door into the Kingdom. The only door. (The thief climbs in some other way and does so to kill and destroy. John 10) It is sometimes hard for us humans to accept this. We tend to think that we need to earn His divine grace. Earn our spot in the kingdom. Earn the "right" to be there, so we try building our own door into the place of rest.

Psalm 23. God wants to give His children a place to rest. A place of shelter. A place to receive nourishment and protection. What a mess it creates for God's people when someone formulates their own works-doorway! When a tired Christian just wants to get in out of the cold for the night and rest in "the barn," when the rain and the wind have beat on us all day and we just need to rest in His provisions, the accusing voice of the door-digger has made a mess there. "You shouldn't rest. See all your fellow Christians out there in the fight? Who do you think you are? You aren't worthy of these provisions. You have more provisions than other Christians. It would make God happier if you suffered more. You need to achieve list A, B, and C before God is pleased and before you deserve to rest."

Don't be a rotten door-digger. God has provided an ample doorway! He gave us the freedom to gladly walk through the doorway and find rest. "I am come that (you) might have life, and that (you) might have it more abundantly." (John 10:10 KJV)

I don't know where in my barn that this hole-chewing critter wants to go once it is inside, but even he has to run through soppy-sloppy manure and water-soaked sawdust because of his own choice of actions.

We *cannot* earn what He has already freely given.

Prayer: Lord, You are my Shepherd. It is You Who makes me lie down in green pastures and beside still waters. You are the One Who restores my soul. Prepare for me today, even in the presence of my enemies, a table. Anoint my head. Fill my cup with abundant, life-giving resources—overflowing with enough to share with others.

(Psalm 23)

Notes

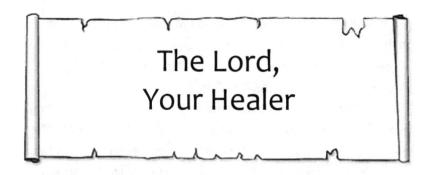

The Lord, Your Healer

Exodus 15:23 (KJV)
"And when they came to Marah, they could not drink the waters of Marah for they were bitter."

Exodus, as we know, holds the story of the grand escape from slavery and the journey to the Promised Land. In Exodus 15 they had just experienced the miracle of the Red Sea opening for them. Now they are in the desert of Shur and can't find water. For three days, they can't find water.

"When they came to Marah, they could not drink the water at Marah because it was bitter. Then the people complained against Moses: 'What are we to drink?' Moses cried out to the Lord, and the Lord showed him a tree, which he threw into the water, and the water became sweet. There the Lord presented to them a statute and an ordinance, and there He tested them. He said, 'If you will carefully obey the Lord your God, do what is right in His eyes, listen to His commandments, and keep all His statutes, then I won't inflict on you all the diseases that I inflicted on the Egyptians, because I am the Lord your healer.'" (Exodus 15:23-26, ISV)

Water tasted bitter. God showed Moses a tree. Tree thrown in the water made the water sweet. Scientifically, this makes no sense! Sometimes my coffee tastes bitter. What if I stuff a tree into my coffee cup? There. That's better.

No, that's just weird, but God has a design for everything, even the things that don't make sense to us at the time. The meaning of the name Marah is bitter. Ever feel bitter? Ever had things happen to you that give you a bitter taste? It's amazing that emotions have a flavor. Things can easily give us a sour attitude or be so hard to take that we feel bitter about it.

I don't know what a tree had to do with making the water sweet. Proverbs 15:4 says, "A wholesome tongue is a tree of life..." (KJV) Maybe this is the tree that takes the bitter taste out. Maybe a willingness to pick up our cross and carry it will repurpose the bitter cup. Maybe for our "bitter waters," it's the log we pull out of our own eye (Luke 6:42) that changes our cup. Maybe in our time, that's the tree we throw in.

At any rate, instead of asking, "Why is this happening to me?" could we rather enter Jesus into our "Marah" and begin to see the shift from bitter to sweet?

Interesting that at this place of bitter waters, God makes a covenant with them to heal them if they obey Him. "I am the Lord your healer," He said. Bitterness could be a sin to repent of, or *maybe* it's a wound we need healing for. Would you consider being kind to yourself and bring the wound to Jesus *to be healed*.

Sometimes the answers don't come from the questions we ask, but from the experience we have.

Prayer: Today, again, like a few other days, I don't wish to assume what you, dear one, may be going through. Let today's prayer flow from your heart and pour it all out to Him. He is The Lord, YOUR healer.

Notes

Called to
Be Free

Galatians 5:13 (NLT)
"For you have been called to live in freedom—not the freedom to satisfy your sinful nature, but the freedom to serve one another in love."

Have you ever thought about how heavy anger, hostility, and jealousy are? The very burden it is to take on the job of monitoring everyone around you?

I am a mother of three. When my children were little, I had to referee a lot of squabbles about who had the most cheerios, who took whose toy, and who had their turn. It's exhausting.

It's also exhausting to carry around strife, envy, and a scale to weigh the words and deeds of the adults in our lives. Sometimes we don't even realize we're doing this, but we're exhausted all the same.

God has called you—called you to be free. What an amazing gift! What a responsibility. What we do with our freedom can affect the people around us.

For good.

For bad.

If the people in our circle are caught in webs of deceit, immorality, and even abusive behaviors, we won't win our battle with them by joining the swamp fight. Instead of striving with them to make them live righteous or striving with them to make them fill our own emptiness, God called us to be free! Free of the weight of all that gunk.

God also did not give us freedom for us to use it as an excuse to do whatever we want, to live selfishly, without regard for others, or to live sinfully. The strange thing is, He gave us freedom so that we might choose to become a servant. God asks us to make a choice to reject our sinful nature, our ego, our impulse to pass judgment, because it frees us!

As servants of God, called to be free, we are to be free of the enslaving power that the works of darkness have on a person. When God sets us free, we freely give to others the fullness given to us by God. Carrying around our large carpetbag of heavy feelings and devices can rob us of the very strength we need to march out of this Valley of the Shadow we are traveling through. With God's help we can even bring our loved ones out of the Valley with us, but we need to drop the suggestions of the enemy and raise our hands in freedom.

God made us free. With a light heart we are free to be good. Free to be at peace. Free to be gentle. Free to love. Free to serve.

Prayer: Lord, take away the cup of noxious stew that I have been feeding myself for too long. I'm trading it in today for the cup of joy You offer me. Teach me to notice when I'm not walking in freedom. Help me detect the odor of a wrong attitude when it arises. Teach me the flavor of Your liberty.

Notes

Peace and Mercy

Galatians 6:15-16 (NET)
"Neither circumcision nor uncircumcision counts for anything; the only thing that matters is a new creation! And all who will behave in accordance with this rule, peace and mercy be on them, and on the Israel of God."

Like a word that has been lit on fire to make itself visible, so was the word "behold" one evening as I read 2 Cor. 5:17.

> "Therefore if any man be in Christ, he is a new creature: old things are passed away; BEHOLD, all things are become new." (KJV)

Behold. Now there's an old word! I don't hear it in common speech. It has a very simple meaning. To see; look. Being lit on fire as it was that evening, it was like a depiction that the new would be something visible. There is and should be a tangible, obvious, different and NEW quality about the newly created soul. To be a Christian <u>means</u> something. The New Creation is something we will behold. Behold, all things are become new.

Peace and mercy.

The two things most people cry out for. I was raised in a culture where the religious ones made rules for this purpose: so that there is peace. Or at least not strife. There wasn't much emphasis on the new creation as long as you followed a set of rules, didn't cause strife, and obeyed the ones who were in charge. Outward things. Like circumcision, external tack-ons don't count for anything.

Peace and mercy.

Cultures bent toward liberalism want mercy (or permission) for everything. In both extremes—in the fixed lines of rules and in the leniency of indulgence—the focus isn't on the newly created change that happens in a person born again. We cannot manipulate and manufacture peace or mercy. "All who behave in accordance to THIS rule..." (verse 16) What rule? The one where the only thing that matters is the new creation. Peace and mercy are on them. Oh! We'll see the change! But not because of count-for-nothing add-ons! And not because you've abolished the whole moral code! I've heard the argument that "it doesn't matter how I live my life!" Oh yes! It does! Behold, all things are become new. Being a Christian means something. We do behold the difference. It's the difference that Jesus creates from the inside out.

And do you know that this is the only verse in the Bible (to my knowledge!) (I looked it up!) that flips a common phrase and says "the Israel of God"? The usual phrase is the God of Israel. This time it's flipped. When the kingdom of heaven invades the soul of man, the man becomes something new and is now "the person" of God. The Anna of God. The (insert your name) of God. The new creation is the kingdom of heaven personified.

Prayer: Lord, forgive me for the times I have not represented You well. Free me from the destructive extremes and draw my attention to the relationship You and I have. Fill my cup today with a fresh serving of peace and mercy. Let me carry Your presence today in all the places I go. If I leave a trail, may it be a trail of lives touched by the kingdom of heaven.

Notes

_____

_____

_____

_____

_____

_____

_____

_____

_____

_____

_____

_____

Seek the Greater

Colossians 3:1 (KJV)
"If ye then be risen with Christ, seek those things which are above, where Christ sitteth on the right hand of God."

Hunger.

Hunger is perhaps the most important human desire—especially in your pursuit of God. Of all the human passions or eagerness to live as Christ asks us to live, hunger tops them all.

"Seek those things…" The voice of my pastor faded in my ears as I opened the Strongs app on my phone to see what the Greek meaning of seek was. It means, seek in order to find. Simple enough, but sometimes the greater meaning is inside of the lesser meaning. We know what it means to seek. Do we know what it means to seek *in order to find?*

The pastor was still speaking, but on the screen of my phone were more words to describe seek: *to seek, by thinking, meditating, reasoning; to enquire into, to seek i.e. require, demand, to crave.*

Crave. Hunger. Hunger for those things which are above. To seek in order to find requires that we must believe a thing exists.

To seek in order to find means that we don't stop seeking when it's difficult. Hunger says I must find it or I will die!

I've wasted a lot of time *wishing* my life was better. Wishing is not seeking. I also had many times when I *desired* victory. Desire, although a step better than wishing, is still not seeking. 1 Corinthians 2:9 has the familiar promise that "Eye has not seen, nor ear heard, nor has it entered into the heart of man, the things which God has prepared for those who love Him." And our verse in Colossians today directs us to seek it.

Honey, if your life is disappointing or as bad as a nightmare, sit up and seek. Stand up and seek. God has so much for you. I don't believe that the better that He has for you is only in heaven. Things are often not what they appear to be on the surface. What your life is now is not what it will be.

Notice the progressive words in the definition. Thinking is good. But thinking alone doesn't get you the desired end. Meditating is great. God can, and often does, show us incredible wisdom during a quiet meditation. My point is that if we try to think and reason with the same set of knowledge that got us into the mess that we're in, then, we're still in the mess. Enquire. If what you have *been* doing isn't working, do some searching. The verse doesn't say, "Sit here and do nothing, while I go get your answers." No, if your eye has not seen and your ear has not heard the liberating directives that the Kingdom of Heaven operates in, then, seek *in order to find*. Seek and keep seeking until you can defeat what has been defeating you. If you're in chaos, depression or great turmoil, turn the meaning of it into something greater. Let the turmoil be the motivation to seek the Kingdom of God until you find it. Seek the greater.

Prayer: Precious Lord, make me hungry for You, for the things You have for me. Let me seek You, and don't let me stop. Don't let me be satisfied, or complacent, or without hope. Help me to desire more.

Notes

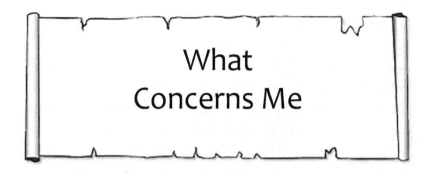

What Concerns Me

Psalm 138:8 (NASB)
"The Lord will accomplish what concerns me; Your loving kindness, O Lord, is everlasting; do not forsake the works of Your hands."

What concerns you today? Take a moment to reflect on the thing that is on your mind.

Where is the Lord in this thing that concerns you? Can you find His hand print? Is the whole thing a mess in need of being thrown out? Or does He want to redeem it for you?

Take a moment to ask Him. Lord, Your loving kindness is everlasting. What is it You'd like to do with this that concerns me?

The verse for today in the literal Hebrew reads like this: "Jehovah will perfect in me." Most of the English translations that I have add phrases to this like, "that which concerns me." "The Lord will fulfill His purpose for me." "The Lord will work out His plan for my life." All these are true, but in Hebrew it simply states that Jehovah Himself will perfect in me. Perhaps if we let that simple phrase sink in, we will see what He's talking about.

He already is perfect. Holy. Whole. How can He perfect in me?

Anxiety is the distress or uneasiness of mind, caused by fear of danger or misfortune. Life doesn't come in neat packages—organized alphabetically. We're born with a natural sense that detects when things are off, wrong, or dangerous. In a real world there is often an overload in this part of our senses. Sometimes our life just takes that turn. We try to stay calm and live in faith. We're called to live by faith, right? But what if a family member is causing some real harm? What if . . . any number of things in real life happen to us? To beat ourselves up for lacking faith only causes more anxiety.

Can I perfect myself? Can I control my universe quite well enough to feel ok? Hardly.

But perhaps if I take a moment to go inward, see where the Lord sits, yes, there He is. He's been with me all along. What I cannot do in all my own effort, He does in me. We give strength and energy to what we focus on. Focus on Jehovah in you. He is loving. Kind, to us. Be kind to yourself today. Let the peace of Him radiate out of your inward part. Enjoy the sense this gives you and watch Him accomplish what concerns you.

Prayer: Oh Lord, Your loving kindness is everlasting. Do not forsake the works of Your hands. *[I] being confident of this very thing, that He which hath begun a good work in [me] will perform it until the day of Jesus Christ."* (Philippians 1:6 KJV)

Notes

Whose Armor
Do I Wear

Romans 10:17 (KJV)
"So then faith cometh by hearing and hearing by the Word of God."

"For they, being ignorant of God's righteousness, and going about to establish their own righteousness, have not submitted themselves unto the righteousness of God." (Romans 10:3 KJV)

Sometimes it can feel like we need to do just that—establish our own righteousness. But the question remains. How can we? "How then shall they call on Him in whom they have not believed? And how shall they believe in Him of whom they have not heard? And how shall they hear without a preacher? And how shall they preach, except they be sent?" (Romans 10:14-15 KJV). In the sequence of verses 14 and 15, the whole process begins where? With us? Hardly! And neither can our righteousness begin with us.

"So then faith cometh by hearing and hearing by the Word of God." Even our faith is not from ourselves!

In some ways people are all the same, and in some ways we are each vastly different and unique. I found it to be a *human* condition to hold a belief that we need to make ourselves good.

From a perspective of habit—the forming of habits—yes, we

are in charge of our lives and our choices are up to us. Absolutely. We need to take responsibility for our lives. We grow up, take charge, and live responsibly. We need to do that. But when it comes to how we stand before God, we can not ever earn our own righteousness!

Nothing to prove.

Isn't it interesting that the word submit is used? There is a pride involved when we have the drive to establish our own righteousness. And there is a movement of humility in submitting to the righteousness of God.

Another interesting observation I have seen in my own life is this: When I strive to constitute my own righteousness, I am wearing my own armor. I'm flying my own flag. Our works are bound to get tested. The Accuser sees the opportunity to harass the tar out of me when I wear my own logo. But when I submit—when I lean in to God and receive His righteousness—I am also covered BY Him. Even though it's the enemy's job to test everything, he sees the surrender to the covering of God and he loses courage.

I relax. The temptations lose their grip. I have nothing to prove.

Faith cometh by hearing. What are you listening to?

Prayer: Lord, forgive me for my ignorance. Create in me a clean heart, O God, and renew a right spirit within me. Cast me not away from Your presence, and take not Your Holy Spirit from me. Restore unto me the joy of Your salvation and uphold me with Thy free Spirit. Let me again experience the joy of Your deliverance and sustain me by giving me the desire to obey! (Psalm 51:10-12)

Notes

Tenacious
Confidence

Hebrews 10:35-36 (NIV)
"So do not throw away your confidence; it will be richly rewarded.
You need to persevere so that when you have done the will of
God, you will receive what He has promised."

What is confidence? Is it being loud and out front? Is it shouting
and arguing to prove that you know a thing? Is it power? Is it a
foundation to stand on? Is it quiet serenity? Is it a promise? Paul
writes here in Hebrews to not throw it away. Maybe it's a small
thing—this confidence—that we can hold in our hand or slip
into our pocket. Paul says not to throw it away and that we will
be richly rewarded. Is confidence, perhaps, like an IRA account
that we invest in, but we don't see the full reward of it until later?

We *will* be tested to various degrees of severity in our lifetime. I dare say we don't know if we *have* confidence until we're
in a trial. I do know that sometimes we have to stand our ground
in the face of suffering. Sometimes we have to hold our confidence quietly as we're publicly insulted. Sometimes we lend our
confidence to those we stand alongside of as *they* suffer. (See
Heb. 10:32-34)

Whether, at times, we have to be vocal in confidence, or, at times, be quiet and only carry our confidence in secret, we must *never* throw it away. The *promise* here is that we *will be* richly rewarded.

Pumpkin, whatever you're going through, PERSEVERE! Do the will of God! All the way through to the end. You will receive what God has promised. You're stronger than you know.

Drink a cup of confidence today and let it strengthen your inner being to endure to the end.

Prayer: Here, again, is my cup, Lord. Today, scoop up some confidence and let me taste it. Let me drink deeply of Your rich strength and let it soak into my very being. Come what may, Lord, You and I will face it together.

Notes

Without Faith It Is Impossible to Please God

Hebrews 11:1 (KJV)
"Now faith is the substance of things hoped for, the evidence of things not seen."

Early in my search for God in one of the hardest trials of my life, I felt the war between faith and doubt waging inside of me. We think we know what faith is until it's tested. Then suddenly in the stark middle of a real-life test, we aren't sure we have any faith at all.

Is faith really that fickle? Does it come and go like a feather in the wind? Is it so imaginary that it can be lost as soon as it is attained? Does faith move the mountain or do we wait until it's moved and then have faith that it was God who moved it?

These questions and more drove me to the Word of God in the search for what faith is. I encourage you to study on your own. You might take a week, or a month, or several months and just dig deep into the Word of God, asking Him to show you what He wants you to know about faith.

My own search took me to James. It's a short book, but it has a lot to say about faith. Hebrews 11 has sometimes been called the Hall of Faith. God showed me that these Heroes, as we call them, were *just people*. They were no different than you and I. What set them apart and what allowed them to do the supernatural and heroic deeds was the element of faith. As you walk through the Hall of Faith in Hebrews 11, you see just inside the front door a plaque on the wall. On the plaque is verse 6: "Without faith it is impossible to please Him: for he that cometh to God must believe that He is, and that He is a rewarder of them that diligently seek Him." (KJV)

A whole book could be written about just that one verse! As I said, the war waging inside of me between doubt and faith drove me to find answers. After many days searching on my own, and searching together with a few trusted friends, discussing at great length the elements of faith, I had "boiled" it down to this verse in Hebrews; "without faith it is impossible to please God."

Today's devotional might take but a few minutes to read and does only a small justice to the great wealth available on the subject, but after many hours, days, and weeks of wrestling this to the ground, I concluded that to carry my tattered bag of doubts around on my back was not only not a good idea, it was also a sin. I say this carefully. I would never label a person a sinner because they have yet to arrive at faith. I'm saying in MY trial and what MY doubts were, it was a sin for me to keep carrying them.

I gladly knelt at the foot of the cross, threw my whole bag down and rose with new hope and belief. Together, God and I were going to move my mountain clean off the face of the earth!

Prayer: Lord, You know my faith and You know where I lack faith. Walk with me today and lead me to the truth of faith. Teach me what is true of faith and what is not. Reveal the treasure of faith as I dig and search.

Notes

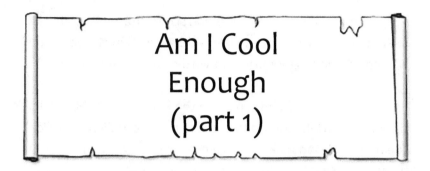

Am I Cool Enough (part 1)

James 2:1 (NIV)
"My brothers, as believers in our glorious Lord Jesus Christ, don't show favoritism."

Today I'd like to discuss the reflection of this verse. We know acutely well the automatic feeling of walking into a room full of people, of giving the speech in front of the class, or of being unprepared with an answer when the teacher calls on you. I doubt that it's only the introverts who feel it. "Am I cool enough?" "Am I cool enough for *them*?" "What do they think of me?" "Are they judging me?"

They might *be* judging me, but why am I thinking this way?

We're familiar with the concept throughout the New Testament of not showing favoritism. Don't judge. Don't think of yourself better than others. Commands that govern the way we treat others. Things we are to do and not to do to others. Have we spent any time scouting out how we allow ourselves to be treated and why?

"Listen to me, dear brothers and sisters. Hasn't God chosen the poor in this world to be rich in faith? Aren't they the ones who will inherit the Kingdom He promised to those who love Him?" (James 2:5 NLT).

The Kingdom of God is not like the kingdoms of this world. Until we get to Revelation 11:15, these two are in direct conflict. To whom did God make the promise? What did He promise to those? The Kingdom. To us. Yet we continually feel inferior to those who lift their chin against us. How is it that our nature is easily inclined to prefer those who do not even prefer us? I see it in myself. I see it in children. I see it in adults. The ones who are "too cool for school" act superior to others and hold themselves aloof, barely give others a glance, withhold affection, punish with cold shoulders those who aren't cool enough. And the inferior of us give preference to those very ones.

My friends, God does not treat us that way! He doesn't behave arrogantly, barely giving us a glance, purposely making us feel shame to dominate us.

He gives!

He gives His *Kingdom* to those who love Him. He sees each of us. Individually. He calls us by our name, and tells us we are His beloved.

Being haughty, judgmental, and showing favoritism are obviously wrong. It's the label in plain sight on the front side of the box, easily discerned as "of this world." But the reflection of the same thing is what we do when we accept inferior labeling. If I walk into a room and am more concerned about what "they" think of me, it's the same bucket of trash from the system of this world. A system we are not even the heirs of! Something we're not to bow to. What we give ourselves to, we become its slave. (Romans 6:16)

The day the Lord showed me this, I tried it. It was so much

fun! I had to do some shopping. I imagined myself free of this trash bucket shackle and walked freely among people. I thought about my inheritance—the Kingdom of Heaven. I thought about how God treats me. I thought about Him feeling the same individual attentiveness to everyone in my town. It was truly liberating and *His* thoughts of my fellowman translated into *my* thoughts of my fellowman.

"My brothers, as believers in our glorious Lord Jesus Christ, don't show favoritism." Also, don't do it to yourself. You are the valuable, blood-bought, honored child of the Living God, and as such, take your place in the world.

Prayer: Jesus, today I want to lay aside the identity the world would like me to wear. Who do You say that I am? Give me images and thoughts today that reflect the true identity You have given me at birth. Exchange what was wrongly assigned to me for what You have designed for me.

Notes

_____

_____

_____

_____

_____

_____

_____

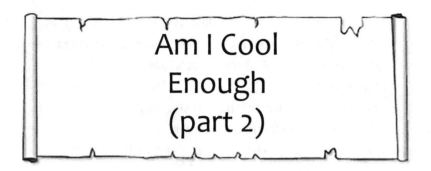

Am I Cool Enough (part 2)

Galatians 5:13 (NIV)
"You, my brothers, were called to be free. But do not use your freedom to indulge the sinful nature; rather serve one another in love."

I had always seen this verse as two separate things. A to-do list of two commands. 1. Don't indulge the sinful nature. 2. Love and serve one another.

In light of the reflection of James 2:1 and yesterday's study, this verse sounds more like: free to love. If we are free of casting people by rank and free of worrying about *being* casted, we're free to love! As the behavior of favoritism and haughty casting is obviously of a sinful nature, so is the reflection of it when we let ourselves be treated this way. If we are in Christ and know who we are (we are promised the whole Kingdom of God), what are we worried about? When we remove, like an unwanted head-shackle, the whole bucket of trash of favoritism from our minds, we are . . . free to love!

When we know and live with knowing that we are the image of God—the One Who pays individual attention to each person—this brings peace. Out of peace, there's love.

Free to love.

Imagine yourself free of the shackle. Imagine yourself as the heir of the whole Kingdom of God. Walk with your chin up. Love like no one is judging. Because at the end of the day, what impresses us, dictates us.

When I feel inferior and I feel under the judgment of people who have set themselves as my superior, it's really hard to love them. I feel more connected to the need to earn *their* love. This is a sickness. This is not who God declares that we are. "You are a chosen people, a royal priesthood, a holy nation, a people to be His very own and to proclaim the wonderful deeds of the one who called you out of darkness into His marvelous light." (1 Peter 2:9 ISV)

We are called to be free. We are to live free of the sinful nature—both in acting superior and in accepting inferior labeling. In freedom we can love like Jesus loves. We can be the change we long to see in the world.

Prayer: Lord, help me walk with the Holy Spirit and not give in to any form of the sinful nature. When I am overcome with the concerns of the flesh, remind me to come running back to You for more of Your Spirit. In my flesh, in my own strength, I cannot make myself a holy person. Only You, Lord, only by Your Spirit, can I be strengthened to walk worthy of You. Do this in me today.

Notes

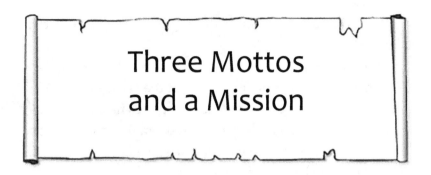

Three Mottos
and a Mission

1 Thessalonians 1:3 (NIV)
"We continually remember before our God and Father your work produced by faith, your labor prompted by love, and your endurance inspired by hope in our Lord Jesus Christ."

One drizzly morning in June, I opened my Bible to Thessalonians. I had only a short time to enjoy my coffee with the Lord before I rushed into my busy summer day. I pondered on the words.

Work produced by faith.

Labor prompted by love.

Endurance inspired by hope in Jesus.

As I wrote this beautiful summary of the Thessalonian people into my journal, I remembered another passage. I looked it up. It's in Micah 6:8. "What doeth the Lord require of thee but to do justly, and love mercy, and to walk humbly with thy God?" (KJV) The lists are remarkably similar!

What an excellent motto to adopt in my life! I held my coffee in both hands and let the aroma awaken my senses. The number one focus in Paul's life was to get the gospel out into all the known world, I thought as the coffee and the Word were waking me up. Then my thoughts turned a different direction.

What if.

What if God put us on the surface of the earth—not for our pleasure, but for a purpose? What if He put us here to take dominion and to push out the dark? To redeem the space. What if He put us here, not to see what life of ease we can create, but put us here on a battlefield to win a war?

The coffee was gone now and I needed to start my day. I looked again at the list I had written in my journal.

Work produced by faith.

Labor prompted by love.

Endurance inspired by hope in Jesus.

Each of the three looked to me like giant sets of parentheses inside of which to place all of our actions. Whatever doesn't fit inside of these three mottos probably isn't important.

Prayer: Lord, engrave these words into my mind that I not forget them.

If I love, let it be with Your love. If I serve, let it be unto You. If I counsel, let it be to set the captive free. If I move, let me be Your hands and Your feet. If I inspire, let me inspire people to move closer to You. If I ignite a soul, let it be with the fire of the Holy Spirit. Fill me with Your Holy Spirit. Fill me. Surround me. May everyone who comes near me feel like they are in the presence of God. Redeem the space that I fill.

Notes

Come Boldly

Hebrews 4:16 (KJV)
"Let us therefore come boldly unto the throne of grace, that we may obtain mercy, and find grace to help in time of need."

"The fear of the Lord is the beginning of wisdom." (Proverbs 9:10)

It's the beginning. A beginning speaks of something coming after it. Our journey is progessive. If we stay at the beginning, stuck at fearing, and never move on to the wisdom and the intimacy of the relationship, we might be afraid to talk to Him. To be open with Him. To trust Him. To tell Him what's really going on.

I spent years feeling so unimportant that I felt like I was annoying God with my needs. Somewhere in my programmed mind I thought that God must be busy doing vital stuff and shouldn't be bothered. Most of the time I would apologize for my needs and basically treat myself like a slave who had no rights.

Every journey has a beginning. If the fear of the Lord is the beginning of wisdom, then, by deduction, it's also not wise to disrespect Him. When we start with a fear and respect for the Creator of the Universe, we can eventually arrive at a place where we can come boldly to Him.

"Let us therefore…"

Why can we come boldly? Because of Jesus. Whether we've been programmed to think we're unimportant or whether we view ourselves as terribly important—neither one counts for anything. It's Jesus. Because of Jesus, we have access.

"Let us therefore come boldly unto the throne…" Ever the curious sort, I looked up the word for boldly here. It means: freedom in speaking; unreservedness in speech; free and fearless; confidence; cheerful courage. Peaches, I encourage you to take inventory of your heart and understand *in what way* you've been bringing your requests to God. "…that we may obtain mercy, and find grace to help in time of need."

Seek and keep on seeking. Don't give up. Your needs, your brand of brokenness, your varied and deeply personal circumstances, the question your heart has been asking—there are answers. Don't stop seeking. There will be obstacles to overcome. You'll overcome them. There will be things to learn. You'll learn them. There will be people to meet. You'll meet them. There *is* help in time of need. Come boldly, with cheerful courage, to the throne of grace. It's not on *your* merit, but His, that you're invited to come.

Prayer: Today, let the prayer grow out of your personal need. Scan your soul for those pesky doubts that keep you from boldly believing and throw them out.

Notes

Heart of Man

Hebrews 8:10 (KJV)
"For this is the covenant that I will make with the house of Israel...I will put my laws into their mind, and write them in their hearts..."

Why did God say that He would put His law in our hearts?

My niece had a tragic disappointment not long ago. It's fresh in my mind. I grieve with her in her sorrow. One day when she and I were talking, I heard these words come out of my mouth: The enemy's purpose in this pain is to get you to close your heart. His purpose is to get you to determine that you will n e v e r open up your heart to that kind of love again. Not for them!

The enemy puts thoughts in our minds like: "It's too painful to love." "I don't want to be hurt again." "I will never make myself available to be betrayed." But the covenant that God makes with us says, "I will put *My* laws in your heart."

Why did He say that?

I have also seen people try to live holy by silencing their heart. I've seen people attempt to conquer temptations by shutting off all feelings. Living holy is a worthy endeavor. I commend a person for having the desire to be holy. God commands it, after all. But why, if our hearts have the power to lead us astray, didn't God say, "I will shut down your heart so that you won't sin against Me?"

I don't know about you and your story, but where I come from there are plenty of people who would have liked to condemn my heart to hell. Not sure why abusers hate our hearts so much, but when our hearts condemn us, the Covenant reframes the story. The rest of Hebrews 8:10 says, "and I will be to them a God, and they shall be to me a people." There is a battle going on for the hearts of men and women.

"For I will be merciful to their unrighteousness, and their sins and iniquities will I remember no more." (Hebrews 8:12 KJV)

When God is my God and I am His person, I belong to His tribe. What does His tribe do when painful things happen at the hands of other people? What should my niece do in her sorrow? The purpose of God in tragedy is very different than the plan of the enemy. God knows all the depths and the heights of feelings and desires within our human heart. And He loves it. With all the flaws and beauty my heart holds, that's the exact spot God chose to set up camp. He knows the enemy is out to steal, kill, and destroy the human heart. God says, "Not on My watch! I will put MY laws in your heart."

When the enemy would want us to harden our hearts, God's law says I will be merciful. I will love anyway. I will love purely. I will keep no record of wrongs. I will forgive because He forgave me. Vengeance belongs to God.

"Above all else, guard your heart, for it affects everything you do." (Proverbs 4:23 NLT) No wonder there is a battle going on for our hearts! I am so glad that God DID say that He will put His laws in my heart!

Prayer: Lord, today I open my broken heart to You. Take out the shame. Soften the stony parts. Make me Yours. Fully. You are my God and I am your person. Set up camp in my heart and put in it all the supply I need to live holy. Like You.

Notes

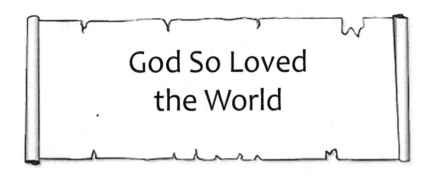

God So Loved
the World

Colossians 3:17 (KJV)
"And whatsoever ye do in word or deed, do all in the name of the Lord Jesus, giving thanks to God the Father by Him."

What if we lived with this motto: Do everything you do with this in mind; For God so loved the world.

Perspective.

A list of love-your-neighbor jobs can seem heavy. Sometimes the commands and directives in the Word of God seem like a long to-do list. Have I done them all? Have I done enough? Have I failed to do a few entirely? Am I lining up or am I mismanaged, not hitting any mark at all? Am I behaving like I imagine a "good" person would?

Trying to *be* good is especially heavy. Trying to be good also often makes us guardians-of-the-list. If we sense that someone is trying to detract from our value or suggest that we aren't as good as we think we are, we get defensive of the list we believe we've assimilated. Sit in your heavenly seat for a minute. (Eph. 2:6) Sit with God and see the earth through His eyes. Do you see it? There is the earth. See the people? Hurrying around, impatient, worried, lonely. Can you feel the compassion He has for the world? It helps to get a perspective from this position.

What if we color our whole day with the perspective we gain from sitting with God? When I take a check to the bank and I have the phrase *for God so loved the world* in my mind, how will I treat the bank clerk? When on my way home the traffic suddenly goes crazy, how will I think towards those other misgoverned drivers if I have in mind that God so loved the world?

Whether I own the business or am the employee, what difference will it make when I keep this phrase in mind? There is no job on this earth that is not affected by our attitude. From building a hotel to being the cleaning staff in a fully built hotel, from the waste manager to the CEO office manager, we all make an impact in the world.

"In Christ, God was reconciling the world to Himself, not counting their trespasses against them, and entrusting to us the message of reconciliation. Therefore, we are ambassadors for Christ, God making His appeal through us. We implore you on behalf of Christ, be reconciled to God." (2 Cor. 5:19-20 ESV)

Prayer: Lord, make me aware that I am Your ambassador today. I will behave this way because of who I am. I won't keep a list to see if I'm being good. I will do all that I do with this in mind: For God so loved the world.

Notes

Author and Perfecter

Hebrews 12:2 (NIV)
"Let us fix our eyes on Jesus, the author and perfecter of our faith, who for the joy set before Him endured the cross, scorning its shame, and sat down at the right hand of God."

The author and perfecter. Who wants perfect faith? I long to have perfect faith. Perfect faith. Never doubting. Never failing. Never wavering between two persuasions. Always true. Always encouraging and positive.

After 25+ years of living the process, I heard a man reading this verse and maybe for the first time in those 25 years, it made sense. Jesus, the author and perfecter. In those three little words is a *lifetime* of meaning. How does Jesus perfect our faith? How is faith made perfect?

The example in the verse is that He endured the cross. How long did that take? One day? The week of His trial and crucifixion? Three years? His whole 33 years on the earth? I'm leaning more toward the whole 33 years. Perhaps longer. Time isn't measured in heaven as it is here and He was designed to be the Savior from the foundation of the world. (1 Pet. 1:19-20) So maybe He *forever* endured the cross. My point is that our faith is not magically perfected in a moment of elated euphoria.

Jesus is not surprised that we take a long time building faith. Enduring the cross, enduring hardships, picking *up* the cross, *deciding* to face adversities—these aren't interruptions to our faith. Again and again we find ourselves in a situation where there's a rock wall on one side and a hard place on the other side. If you're anything like me, you immediately begin to question how you managed to "fail" again. "Why am I here?" "What did I do wrong?" "How can I get out of this mess?"

In the half second that it took the man to read these words, I saw a lifetime of hard situations and I understood this verse. Jesus IS the author and the PERFECTER of our faith. The trials are not designed to bring us to ruin. They're designed to bring us close.

"Humble yourselves therefore under the mighty hand of God, that He may exalt you in due time." (1 Pet. 5:6 KJV) Again, a lifetime of meaning in three words—in due time.

"If ye abide in Me, and My words abide in you, ye shall ask what ye will, and it shall be done unto you." (John 15:7 KJV) Abiding is a lifetime. It's a word that means to remain. Not a quick stop. Not an overnight stay. We're in for the long haul and the perfecting of our faith means there will be reasons to HAVE faith. A weightlifter has no idea how strong he is until he tests his strength. We may or may not know if we have any faith at all until it gets tested.

You haven't failed. This is not the end of you. It's all part of life. Grab your cross, fix your eyes, and decide to finish this thing well!

Prayer: Lord, make my cup of broth today be one of abiding relationship with You that I will have the strength to endure and conquer these tests that I'm in and headed for. Make me, in due time, see the good You are working in me.

Notes

A Dad and Two Sons

Luke 15:12 (KJV)
"And the younger of them said to his father, 'Father, give me the portion of goods that falleth to me.' And he divided unto them his living."

The story of the Prodigal Son has been squeezed into every theological shape I can think of!

Apparently the man had two sons and these two boys each had a completely different outlook on the meaning of life. I have heard many wonderful conclusions as to what Jesus was trying to tell us through this story. And like the two sons, the people that have told these conclusions have had different outlooks on what the story means.

One day recently I was, again, listening to someone read this passage. This time my mind caught verse 31. I'm sorry for the person reading because they continued reading, but I stopped listening.

"My son," the father said, "you are always with me, and everything I have is yours." (NIV)

You are always with me and everything I have is yours. Stop. What?

Let's lay aside the fact that the elder son was having a bad attitude. Focus on the words the father says to his boy, the son, made in his image, and born into his family. "You are always with me. Everything I have is yours."

The Literal Translation Bible says, "Child, you are always with me, and all of my things are yours."

Earlier in the story we are told that the young son wanted his share, was given it, and he went out and spent it. It says the father *divided* unto them. So, when the young son got his portion, the elder son got what was his own as well. But in verse 31 the father says, "All of my things are yours!"

Most people agree that the metaphoric Dad here is God and the sons are us. Where was the elder son? He stayed on the farm. He stayed with God. He worked in the field. He was living in the Kingdom. If the father in this story is God, what does God have? I mean, really! What. Does. God. Have?

The young son went out, away, distant, on his own, spending his gifts and possessions apart from relationship with his dad. The resources ran out.

The elder son stayed.

Where am I? If I'm a child of God, living in the Kingdom, what am I doing with a bad attitude? Why am I living like I had a limited amount of Kingdom resources? Why are my prayers mixed with the stench of doubt—pig food?

All I have is yours. Child, *all* I have is yours. All?

Pick up your head, Blueberry! Look at your location. I mean, for real. If you're *not* in the Father's house, close to Him, working with Him, then, arise and go there! But if you're already there . . . My goodness, you don't have only *your* gifts, talents, and resources, but also all that the Father has is yours!

I think we live *f a r* beneath our potential. What are we doing there? Arise. Go. There's a feast going on. There's plenty. You're not just invited. You belong.

Prayer: *Our Father which art in Heaven. Hallowed be Thy name. Thy Kingdom come. Thy will be done. As in Heaven. So on earth.* Bring this truth into my reality. Render me wide open and extend my faith to embrace this abundant resource.

Notes

Fully Equipped

Ephesians 3:19 (ESV)
"And to know the love of Christ that surpasses knowledge, that you may be filled with all the fullness of God."

"Paul, after staying many more days in Corinth, said farewell to the brothers and sailed away to Syria accompanied by Priscilla and Aquila." (Acts 18:18 NET)

Imagine with me the scene in this verse. Imagine the scent of water and wet sand. The crunch of the pebbles and rocks under the feet of the Apostle Paul as he approaches the ship. People calling out to each other. The captain yelling orders to the oarsmen. The bang and thunk of supplies and barrels as the crew loads the bay. These sailors sail every day. They know what they need on a trip and they're loading the ship with all the things they need. In our imagination we can see them carry aboard the crates and bundles of merchandise to sell at their next stop.

Imagine being on the sea for days and weeks at a time. Imagine the supplies necessary for a long voyage. Food—for all persons aboard. Water to drink. Extra ropes. The fishing equipment. (I imagine fish would have been part of the menu while sailing.) Watch with me as these supplies are carried in. Perhaps we can see a portable, earthen oven on board. See, here comes a boy, carrying firewood for the galley.

See the marines over there packing up the ammunition? Enemy ships and pirates were a common threat. The captain of this ship is prepared with trained men to guard and protect his ship and crew.

We can imagine the sounds of the sail fabric as it flaps in the breeze, waiting for the big, burly sailors to pull up the heavy anchors. Imagine the oarsmen, walking single file, up the boarding plank. Their feet are bare, but we can hear the creaking of the long, wooden walk plank under their weight. Imagine the first one walking with his head down, concentrating on the task at hand. Imagine the second one glancing at us, wondering what two strangers are doing there, staring at them like we've never seen a ship before. Imagine the last guy in the line of oarsmen, looking around as he follows in line, his eyes taking in every bit of landscape before he disappears into the ship's bottom deck.

The ship is now fully stocked, fully supplied with the manpower they need, with the sailing equipment they need, with soldiers, and the proper ammunition. Everything is ready.

"All aboard!" shouts the captain. "Take up the anchors!" We listen to the rumble of the rusty anchors as the muscled sailors drag them up the wooden sides of the ship. And off they go! We can hear the splashing and the churning of the water as the oars take the ship out into deeper water and the stronger winds.

They are fully loaded and prepared for the voyage. This fullness is the word Paul uses in Ephesians 3:19, when he says "that you may be filled with all the fullness of God."

Paul prayed some powerful prayers in chapter one as well as in chapter three. Today my mind is blown with the imagery of what this word holds! It's not a distant fullness, far removed and irrelevant to us! It's a fullness *OF EVERYTHING THAT WE NEED!* Fully equipped. Fully stocked. Fully staffed for the calling to which He has called us to. This is the will of God!

Skipper, we are not left on our own and helpless! Why are we often living life like it's all up to us?!

Prayer: Oh my heavenly Father! I pray with Paul that I will be strengthened with power through the Holy Spirit in my inner being! I thank You that I am rooted in love, grounded in love, and that You will show me the breadth, height, and depth of this love of Christ that surpasses knowledge. I ask you, almighty God, to fill me with the *fullness* of God! Make me aware of it as I walk the walk You have given me. Amen.

Notes

Meet My Friend Zechariah

Luke 1:19 (NET)
"The angel answered him, 'I am Gabriel, who stands in the presence of God, and I was sent to speak to you and to bring you this good news.'"

It was Christmas. I was looking through the story in the first chapter of Luke. The angel Gabriel was the messenger to both sets of parents. I mean, Gabriel, folks! The one who stands in the presence of God and the one who appears to humans when the big deals get made! Maybe Zechariah, Joseph, and Mary didn't know him. Could be. He doesn't appear often.

What I noticed was the response of Zechariah, and the response of Mary. When the angel told Zechariah about the son he would soon have, he told Zechariah not to give him strong drink because of the great work his boy would be born to do, and what his important job would be. It was a clear and detailed word, not a subtle impression. It was clearly worded and specific.

Zechariah's response? "Whereby shall I know this?" He also reminded the angel how old he and his wife were. And because he didn't believe the message, Zechariah was made unable to speak until the baby was born and named. This could have been partly a punishment and partly mercy. Mercy, in that it kept him from further talking himself out of the promise, but also punishment because of his unbelief. And yet, there's something I learned from Zechariah.

When the angel came to Mary, she also asked questions but on a closer study of the words, I found that the two responses are, in fact, two different words.

Zechariah's response was *kat-ah*. His question back to the angel could be said another way—"How the heck do you expect me to believe this?"

Mary asked *pos*, an adverb, meaning *in what way*. Essentially, she said, "Okay, this will happen. In what way will this happen?"

To give Zechariah credit, I imagined how life had gone for him. Verse 6 says that both he and his wife were righteous before God, walking blamelessly in all the commandments and ordinances of the Lord. And yet the one thing they wanted was denied them. That had to have been intensely disappointing. They were childless for one month, two months, three months, one year, two years, and then it was many, *many* years! When the angel finally came with the news of a son, they were very old. In all these years, Zechariah could have cycled through many days of trying to encourage himself only to hit the bottom of disappointment. Again and again. Until he was finally resigned to what he believed to be his lot in life. I couldn't criticize him for his unbelief!

Mary was young and perhaps naïve and full of fresh dreams of the future. Maybe it's easy to grab on to the promise of an angel message at that stage of the game. Zechariah had a much harder time. So I wonder, gentle soldier, what can we do to keep our hearts tender?

In all the long, hard struggles we face, how can we keep a tender, open posture to the Word of the Lord? Guarding our hearts, tending to the wellness of our emotions, are perhaps more important than we thought. If one prayer doesn't get answered, can we get busy seeking the Lord in other areas? If we're disappointed, can we stay sweet?

Can we keep blame and bitterness out and instead embrace a new choice? Disappointment is hard on us. Very hard. It can turn a hopeful young man into a cynical one who can't even believe an Angel who physically shows up to tell him he will get the very thing he had prayed for his whole life. Take care of your soul, my friend. Look for every opportunity to see hope and new choices, new ways to serve, new horizons to explore.

Prayer: Lord, there is nothing that happens to me that is so bad that I can't stay sweet. This is true when I stay filled with Your Spirit. Fill me now. Fill me as I sit and wait for You.

Notes

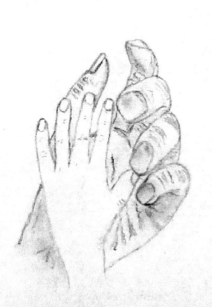

Meet My Friend Zechariah, Part 2

Luke 1:17 (NIV)

"And he will go on before the Lord, in the spirit and power of Elijah, to turn the hearts of the fathers to their children and the disobedient to the wisdom of the righteous. To make ready a people prepared for the Lord."

We've already established that Zechariah was an old man and that he had gotten himself into a state of cold indifference, cynical and disappointed in life.

Watch the sequence of what happened in Zechariah's story. Hopeful young man, years of disappointment, cynical view of supernatural possibilities, angel visits, coldhearted man doubts the angel, spends nine months "pregnant" with the promise of the miracle baby with Elizabeth, man births the promise—the baby that will operate in the spirit of Elijah.

This moves me a great deal! Have you ever been around maybe an aunt or uncle, grandparent or elderly friend, who has a darkened view of the world? There are a few of those in my life. Everything is going to hell, according to them. People are bad, and getting worse. Children are horrible imbeciles with no sense. This is how they talk, and what they talk about. It's rather depressing to be around them. Guess how much influence such a heart has on turning the disobedient to wisdom, and fathers to their children. I know I, for one, don't want to hear anything they have to say!

How can the older generation reach the young? How can Grandmother stay interesting to Grandchild and pass along a lifetime of wisdom? How can Uncle teach Nephew the strength of manhood? How can Grandfather teach young Christian the fruits of the Kingdom?

We could say that we "give birth" to more than just children. We birth ideas. We birth plans. We birth new companies, new movements, even revivals.

When Zechariah "gave birth" to the "spirit of Elijah" he watched in astonishment as his "mouth" was "opened." He began to speak. He spoke praises. Luke 1:67-80 is a fascinating account of what came out of his mouth! No longer was our friend a sullen, bitter, and irrelevant old guy.

Verse 65 says, "The neighbors were filled with awe, and throughout the hill country of Judea people were talking about all these things."

What are the dreams inside of you? What ambition has lain dormant, perhaps for years and years? I encourage you, get them out of storage! Dust off those aspirations and ask the Lord for a fresh anointing. He might want to renew old dreams. He might want to give you a new dream. Don't give up. Don't ever give up the hope of a better future! God is already there. He was in the past. He's in the present day and He's already in the future. Together with Him and a renewed mind, you can birth whatever promise He's given you. When that "child" is born, watch "a people be prepared for the Lord!"

Prayer: Lord, I don't want to be bitter and irrelevant when I am old. The next generation needs me. Stir in me a "Spirit of Elijah" that is fresh and powerful in the turning of hearts to You and to each other. Help me be a conduit and not a dismal grouch.

Notes

Posture Is Everything

Luke 22:20 (NIV)
"In the same way, after the supper He took the cup, saying, 'This cup is the New Covenant in my blood, which is poured out for you.'"

"I invite you all to come up, get the elements, and return to your seat; we'll partake together."

These are familiar words at our local church. Communion has loads of special meaning for me. It's holy. It's ceremony. It's celebration. It's somber. It's unifying. It's many things and it's one of the things Jesus instructed us to do. Its symbolism teaches us many things. One person's revelation through communion doesn't detract from another person's revelation.

Last Sunday as I was sitting with our congregation, elements in hand, listening to the instructions, I was moved with love as I gazed over the sea of faces around me.

"This is my body, broken . . ."

I saw all of us, in unison, bow our heads and receive the bread from our hands.

"This cup is the New Covenant . . ."

I watched in awe as all of us, together, lifted our heads to drink from the little cups we held.

Everything has meaning. There are patterns in life. His body was broken. We break too. In a broken world we often bow beneath the weight of suffering. Our congregation bowed to receive the bread. He bowed beneath the weight of the world. Not all suffering is good but some of it is necessary. Posture is important.

If the cup is the New Covenant, and *volumes* have already been written about what is in this New Covenant, I will only mention one point here. "We are more than conquerors through Him that loved us." (Romans 8:37 KJV)

The physical activity of drinking from a cup requires that we tip our heads up and back to receive the liquid we're drinking. In other words, to drink from The Cup, we have to lift our heads.

If you're bowed down, is it because you are submitting to some necessary suffering? Or is it a bowing born of defeat and dejection? Both the bowing and the lifting are part of the sacrament. But defeat and dejection never is. "Now the God of hope fill you with all joy and peace in believing, that ye may abound in hope, through the power of the Holy Ghost." (Romans 15:13 KJV) Posture is everything.

Suffer today if you must, but tomorrow lift up your head and take in the Promise of the New Covenant. You are a child of the living God and "His divine power has given us everything we need for life and godliness." (2 Peter 1:3 ISV) Don't buy the lie that all suffering is good. The New Covenant brings the promise of a lifted face. Drink The Cup and look at Him, expectant of the good things He is giving you. "Lift up your tired hands, then, and strengthen your trembling knees! Keep walking on straight paths, so that the lame foot may not be disabled, but instead be healed." (Hebrews 12:12-13 GNB)

Posture is everything.

Prayer: Lord You are holy and You are beautiful. I accept the breaking and the lifting. Bless me as I lift my face to you. Fill me with hope, joy, and peace. I believe that you have made me to be an overcomer.

Notes

Chosen

The Worm

Isaiah 41:14 (KJV)
"Fear not, thou worm Jacob, and ye men of Israel; I will help thee, saith the Lord and thy redeemer, the Holy One of Israel."

For many years I read this verse with my American mind and thought the Lord was calling Jacob a wretch, a maggot of humanity. I read it to mean that even though Jacob was so menial, God still benevolently would come to his rescue.

Until I looked it up.

In the context of the rest of the chapter where God is definitely not casting Jacob as the scum of the earth. Let's look at the word.

Verse 8 and 9; "But thou, Israel, art my servant, Jacob whom I have chosen, the seed of Abraham my friend. Thou whom I have taken from the ends of the earth, and called thee from the chief men thereof, and said unto thee, thou art my servant; I have chosen thee, and not cast thee away." Verse 14; "Fear not, thou worm Jacob . . ."

Turns out that the word used for worm is a *coccus ilicis*, or the scarlet dye made from the dried body of the female *coccus ilicis*. Turns out this Crimson worm is common to the regions of ancient Israel. The color scarlet is significant on many levels but especially because it denotes royalty, and all of this puts a very different light on this verse!

God is telling Jacob that he was born for a purpose! A purpose so great that he is like the ink used to write history! A world-changer!

Has the enemy or those around you been minimizing you and telling you of your insignificance? What are the phrases running in the constant chatter of your mind? Are you in touch with the declarations God has declared over you? Or do you see yourself as a crawling grub, too meager to matter. (We can be our own worst critic at times!)

Shortcake, we. are. so. much. more! Listen to verse 15 in the Easy English version; "Watch this happen! I will cause you to become like a machine that threshes [thresh: get the good part of a plant and throw away the chaff]. It will be new and sharp, with many sharp metal points that are like teeth. You will thresh the mountains and you will break the hills. They will become like chaff [chaff: dead part of a plant round the seed]."

Are you faced with a problem so big it seems like a mountain? God says He will turn you into the very instrument that takes the mountain apart. Again—we participate in our own deliverance.

The good and the bad of each situation can gray together sometimes—especially while we're in it! But God says He will make us like a threshing machine—the instrument that separates the good from the bad. The instrument used to reap a harvest!

This is what He said to Jacob.

This is what He says to you and to me.

You, Baby Bean, are God's chosen. The seed of Abraham. Called to a purpose. You're not a crawling worm! You are ink! Scarlet dye that God uses to write meaning and value into the pages of history. You are the very essence of a world-changer!

"I will help thee, saith the Lord."

Prayer: Creator of heaven and earth, I bow my heart to You. You have chosen me and not cast me away. Make me into a "threshing machine" that knows how to shut out the voice that speaks of dead things, chaff, and instead listens to the voice that calls me to rise up, to conquer, to harvest a crop of good seed! Make me _____ (insert your name), the one who obeys the call.

Notes